HITLER

A BEGINNER'S GUIDE

NIGEL RODGERS

Hodder & Stoughton

A MEMBER OF THE HODDER HEADLINE GROUP

NIAGARA FALLS PUBLIC LIBRARY

COMMUNITY CENTRE BRANCH LIBRARY

Orders: please contact Bookpoint Ltd, 130 Milton Park, Abingdon, Oxon OX14 4SB. Telephone: (44) 01235 827720, Fax: (44) 01235 400454. Lines are open from 9.00–6.00, Monday to Saturday, with a 24-hour message answering service. Email address: orders@bookpoint.co.uk

British Library Cataloguing in Publication Data
A catalogue record for this title is available from The British Library.

ISBN 0 340 80419 X

First published 2001
Impression number   10 9 8 7 6 5 4 3 2 1
Year 2007 2006 2005 2004 2003 2002 2001

Copyright © 2001 Nigel Rodgers

All rights reserved. This is work is copyright. Permission is given for copies to be made of pages provided they are used exclusively within the institution for which this work has been purchased. For reproduction for any other purpose, permission must first be obtained in writing from the publishers.

Cover photo by Bettman/Corbis
Typeset by Transet Limited, Coventry, England.
Printed in Great Britain for Hodder & Stoughton Educational, a division of Hodder Headline Plc, 338 Euston Road, London NW1 3BH by Cox & Wyman, Reading, Berks.

NIAGARA FALLS PUBLIC LIBRARY

COMMUNITY CENTRE BRANCH LIBRARY   MAY - - 2005

CONTENTS

Childhood and youth

No ruler had a greater or more disastrous impact on the twentieth century than Hitler, whose name has become a byword for the evils of dictatorship. Although he failed in all his aims – except the mass murder of European Jews – he indisuputably affected the course of world history. What is most remarkable about Hitler's life is how inadequate he was as a human being in any normal sense. Without the exceptionally disturbed circumstances of Germany after the First World War, he would probably have remained a self-obsessed, paranoid failure. But when imperial Germany and Austria disintegrated after defeat in 1918, Hitler emerged from among their ruins. 'It must be unique in history for someone like me to have got so far,' he mused in 1939, near the peak of his power. However, he did not start from the gutter as he implied in *Mein Kampf* (My Struggle), the often misleading autobiographical manifesto he compiled in 1924.

Hitler's family was neither markedly impoverished nor at all distinguished. Instead it was typical of many families of minor officials serving the Austro-Hungarian Empire which stretched from Italy to Poland. Much about Hitler's ancestry and early life remains obscure, however. His father Alois was born in 1837 the illegitimate son of Maria Schicklgruber, a peasant's daughter. Hitler's paternal grandfather remains unknown even today. Alois was brought up partly by his uncle Nepomuk Hiedler (or Hüttler). At the age of 37, Alois changed his surname from Schicklgruber to Hitler in 1876, possibly to please his uncle Nepomuk– who might conceivably have been his actual father and from whom he may have expected a legacy. All this remains uncertain but suggestions that Hitler's grandfather was Jewish, later repeated by his enemies, can be dismissed. There were no Jews in that part of Austria at the time, for they were forbidden to settle there.

Alois Hitler was upwardly mobile. Joining the imperial Austrian customs service in 1855, he became Higher Collector of Customs Inspector by 1892, a respectable post for someone with little education. But he was personally restless, often changing house – 11 times in 25 years – and wife. Hitler's mother, Klara Pölzl, 23 years his junior and a second cousin, was his third wife (his second died), whom he married in January 1885. Their first three children died in infancy but their fourth, Adolf, born on 20 April 1889, survived, although their fifth did not. At that point the Hitler family was stationed at Braunau, on the Austro-German border, a providential birthplace for one who would unite the two countries, Hitler later claimed. But in 1892 Alois was transferred to Passau and on again to Linz, well inside Austria, in 1894.

In public Alois was a respectable member of society, but at home he was an overbearing husband and a violent or absent father – he preferred drinking in the inn to his family's company. Described by her doctor, as 'simple, modest and kindly', Klara was awed by her husband, crushed by the deaths of so many of her children but loved by the two who survived, especially by her only son, Adolf. Family photographs show a subdued, frightened-looking woman, while Alois, resplendent in his uniform, exudes complacency. Adolf's younger sister, Paula, remembered her mother as a 'very soft and tender person' and she was the only human being whom Hitler genuinely loved. He kept a portrait of her by him until his death. He feared, not loved, his father, who beat him almost every day, according to Paula. Violent, autocratic fathers with cowering wives were not uncommon at the time, but such a background probably encouraged Hitler's admiration for the 'excessive' or 'perverted' masculinity so marked in Nazism.

Adolf first went to school in Lambach, a small town where his father had bought a farm and there he won high marks. In 1898 the family moved again – Alois was now retired – to near Linz, which became their final home. Adolf seems to have done well at this elementary school too, becoming a leader in the wargames the boys played and an avid reader of American Westerns, which remained a lifelong passion.

All his life too Hitler loved Linz, which he regarded as his hometown, the most 'German' town in the polyglot Austrian empire. In 1900 he started secondary school in Linz itself, which meant an hour's walk there and back every day. Here he did much worse, twice having to retake maths and French exams, never being marked as more than 'adequate' in anything except drawing and gym. The long journeys to school cannot have helped his education, but laziness combined with arrogance, recurring features in his life, were the cause of his failures, not lack of ability.

At home, relations with his father worsened. Alois, determined that his son should follow him into the civil service, showed him round the customs offices. Adolf, horrified at the prospect of spending his life in an office, declared he wanted to be an artist. 'Artist! No, never as long as I live!' declared Alois (Hitler, Adolf *Mein Kampf*, 1939). But he did not live long, dying suddenly of a heart attack or stroke in January 1903. He left his family quite comfortably off – Klara had a good widow's pension – and Adolf the only man in the household. Soon Adolf found he could bully his weakly doting mother, principally into letting him leave school early. Klara at first objected but Adolf was only promoted to the next grade in summer 1904 on condition that he then left the school. He went to another school briefly in Steyr, 50 miles away, boarding – a sign of the family's solvency – but by the autumn of 1905, when he was 16, his schooling was over. Hitler later looked back on his schooldays and schoolteachers, and all those who passed exams, with 'elemental loathing' for this, his first rejection.

Hitler now began living the life he always enjoyed most: that of an idle dreamer. With a comfortable room in his mother's apartment in Linz, to which the family had moved, he could spend the day reading, daydreaming, drawing – usually grand buildings – visiting the theatre and opera at night. He looked quite dapper with an ivory-topped walking stick, and his mother even bought him a grand piano for him. His companion at the time, August Kubizek, son of a leather tanner, listened enrapt to his monologues about the evils of teachers and the wonders of German art, especially the music of Wagner, whom Hitler already adored with almost religious fervour. Early in 1906 Hitler visited Vienna for the first time, marvelling at its great boulevards and its opera, both eclipsing those in provincial Linz. In the summer of 1907 he decided to move permanently to the capital as an art student, boosted by a 'loan', really a gift, of 924 kronen from his aunt Johanna – then about a young lawyer's annual salary.

Hitler sat the arduous exams for the Austrian Academy of Fine Arts in September, passing the first tests. Out of 113 candidates, only 28 were finally accepted so his rejection was neither shameful nor unusual, but he was stunned. 'It struck me as a bolt out of the blue,' he said later. The Academy suggested that he study architecture instead, a reasonable suggestion as his best surviving sketches are of buildings, but, lacking the required school qualifications, he could not do so. Instead, he kept quiet about his failure. Meanwhile his mother was dying of breast cancer. Hitler returned to Linz and nursed her 'indefatigably' through her last days, according to Dr Bloch, the family doctor. When Klara Hitler died on 21 December 1907, Hitler was overwhelmed. 'I have never seen anyone so prostrate with grief as Adolf Hitler,' recalled the doctor (Bloch, Edward *My Patient Hitler*, 1941). Years later Hitler would, with unusual gratitude, remember this doctor and let him leave Nazi-occupied Austria without hindrance. Dr Bloch was Jewish.

Early in 1908 Hitler returned to Vienna, alone but hardly impoverished, for he still had some of his aunt's 'loan' and an orphan's 'pension' of 25 kronen a month. The capital of the polyglot Habsburg empire was at its intellectual and artistic zenith: the painter Klimt, Freud, the poet Hofmannsthal, the playwright Schnitzler, the architect Otto Wagner and composer Schoenberg made it the most culturally vibrant German-speaking city. Hitler, however, ignored them in favour of the city's older imperial splendours. But behind Vienna's glittering façade of opulent cafés and restaurants lay some of the worst poverty and slums in Europe, just as beneath the august figure of Franz Josef, Emperor since 1849, the ancient empire was beginning to fall apart. Proclamations of imperial unity could not disguise growing tensions between Germans and other subject nationalities – Italians, Czechs, Poles, Croats, Slovenes, Romanians – or the deepening divisions between the classes.

But one people throughout the Habsburg domains still supported the empire: the Jews. Vienna had the highest concentration of Jews of any major European city – 8.6 per cent of the population. Some, like Freud, Mahler or the Wittgenstein family, from which the great philosopher came, were brilliantly successful and appeared fully assimilated, but others had arrived in Vienna only recently from Poland or Russia. With their long beards, tall hats and 'kaftans' they looked outlandish to Viennese eyes. These poorer Jews congregated in Vienna's old city, especially the north, where Hitler too for a time lived. 'One day, passing through the Inner City, I suddenly encountered a phenomenon in a long caftan and wearing black sidelocks. My first thought was: is this a Jew? ... Whenever I went I now saw Jews, and the more I saw, the more sharply they set themselves apart in my eyes from the rest of humanity,' he wrote in a famous *Mein Kampf* passage, describing with excited disgust his first sight of such Jews. 'The black-haired Jew lies in wait for hours on end ... glaring at and spying on the unsuspicious girl he plans to seduce, adulterating her blood.' (Hitler, Adolf *Mein Kampf*, 1939)

Exactly when Hitler became an obsessive, pathological anti-Semite remains uncertain, but it was after he had left Linz, for there were few Jews there. In 1909 Hitler watched the funeral procession of Karl Lueger, who had been the highly popular and rabidly anti-Semitic mayor of Vienna. Hitler clearly absorbed Lueger's anti-Semitic ideas, noting also the way Lueger's Christian Socialist Party, assisted by the popular press, manipulated and mobilized the masses against the Emperor who despised anti-Semitism. Hitler in turn despised the multiracial Habsburg empire served faithfully by his father. Instead, like many younger Austrians, he looked to Germany – united only since 1871 but now the dominant power in Europe – for redemption in a great pan-German state. In this 'Greater Germany', Jews would have no place.

Hitler picked up other anti-Semitic nationalist ideas from Georg von Schönerer's Pan-German Nationalists, but disagreed with Schönerer's attacks on the Catholic Church, not because of his own faith – he was no Christian – but because such attacks divided popular attention. 'The art of leadership', he wrote in *Mein Kampf*, 'lies in concentrating the people's attention on a single enemy, and ensuring that nothing divides their attention.' He also realized that the Pan-Germans were too narrowly middle class to be a successful mass movement, unlike the Social Democrats, whose huge, impressively organized demonstrations – but not ideas – he admired. A more mystical influence was that of the ex-monk, Adolf Lanz. Lanz's trashy magazine *Ostara* prophesied a blond super-race would rule the world, crushing democracy, feminism and dark-haired people, taking the swastika, an ancient sun-sign, as their symbol. But few people blamed Jews for all their personal misfortunes as well as public ills as Hitler was to do.

Hitler intended to reapply to the Fine Arts Academy in the autumn of 1908; meanwhile he simply idled. Kubizek joined him in February, winning admission to the Vienna Music Conservatory, and the two shared a room. Hitler seldom got up before noon when Kubizek returned from the Conservatory to practise on his piano. Hitler then vanished to visit museums or wander the streets. He took his friend round Vienna, enthusing over its architecture, frequenting the opera – he later claimed to have heard *Tristan und Isolde*, Wagner's erotic masterpiece, 40 times. Hitler himself at this time showed no interest in women. He was probably too seedy and self-obsessed to impress most women, and he recoiled in horror from the prostitutes who abounded in the capital, lecturing Kubizek on the dangers of syphilis and the need for men to remain celibate until their 25th birthday. Kubizek regarded Hitler as deeply misogynistic but not homosexual. (Some writers have attempted to explain his pathological anti-Semitism and later manic instability by suggesting that he caught syphilis from a Jewish prostitute, but there is absolutely no evidence for this.)

Yet Hitler also impressed his friend with his seemingly immense knowledge of architecture, history and music, at one stage planning a Wagnerian opera on the story of Wieland the Smith, for which Kubizek would write the music. Nothing came of this typically grandiose project. In September 1908 Hitler tried again for the Academy, failing even the preliminary test this time. All his hopes ruined, he cut himself off from Kubizek and his family in wounded pride. With his capital exhausted, he moved to progressively shabbier rooms and by late 1909 was living in a doss house. His claims to have worked as a manual labourer are probably false, but he certainly experienced acute poverty at this time. Early in 1910 he moved to a men's hostel close to the Danube, where he lived for his last three years in Vienna. There he met Reinhold Hanisch, a tramp from Bohemia, who encouraged him to paint postcard-sized views of Vienna which Hanisch then sold. The two soon fell out, Hitler accusing Hanisch of cheating him. Hanisch's description of Hitler at the time – dirty old overcoat, greasy black hat, long ragged hair, thin hungry face covered with a black beard – ends by describing him as 'an apparition such as rarely occurs among Christians' presumably meaning that he looked Jewish.

Hitler used to harangue whoever would listen to him in the hostel with his views on Germany (good), priests, Habsburgs, Social Democrats and Jews (all bad). He struck most listeners as unbalanced not because of what he said – his views were commonplace – but because of the fanaticism with which he expounded them. He later said how in these years 'a view of life and definite outlook on the world took shape in my mind. These became the granite basis of my conduct ... Vienna... taught me the most profound lessons of my life' (Hitler, Adolf *Mein Kampf*, 1939). In May 1913 he finally inherited the modest sum of 819 kronen from his father's estate and at once quit Vienna for Munich, a true 'German' city.

2 A brave soldier

Hitler said in *Mein Kampf* that he left Vienna because 'my inner aversion to the Habsburg state was increasing daily' and Munich attracted him because of its art galleries, but he was an autobiographical liar. In truth, he had a far stronger reason for leaving Austria in 1913 (not 1912, as he wrote): to avoid military service in the Austrian army. He should have reported in 1910 for this but loathed the idea of fighting for the Habsburg empire. Pursued by the Austrian authorities even in Bavaria, he finally had to appear before a military tribunal in Salzburg in Austria in February 1914, where, after making a grovelling apology, he was found unfit for service.

At this time he described himself as an 'architectural painter'. Hitler called his first years in Munich 'by far the happiest time of my life ... A *German* city. How different from Vienna.' But in reality he continued with the same aimless way of life as in Vienna, peddling his paintings, arguing politics in cafés and beerhalls with anyone who would listen – mostly about the need for a Greater Germany to incorporate all Germans wherever they lived – and making no real friends. Again he totally ignored the latest intellectual and artistic developments, principally the *Blaue Reiter* (Blue Rider) school of art, which made Munich Vienna's cultural rival. Instead he admired the indisputably fine neoclassical buildings of the previous century, with their grand boulevards and porticos.

Hitler was rescued from this drifting life by the outbreak of war in August 1914. Austro-Hungary had invaded Serbia, using as a pretext the assassination of the Austrian Archduke Ferdinand by Serbians in Sarajevo on 28 June. Russia then came to Serbia's aid, Germany honoured its alliance with Austro-Hungary and France honoured its own alliance with Russia. When Germany, attacking France, violated

Belgian neutrality long guaranteed by Britain, Britain too entered the conflict. The First World War or Great War, the bloodiest until then in human history, was greeted at its onset by cheering crowds in every combatant country, among them Adolf Hitler. The ghastly experience of modern fighting was to change most men's initial enthusiasm into the opposite – but not Hitler's.

'Overpowered by stormy enthusiasm, I fell down on my knees and thanked Heaven from an overflowing heart for granting me the good fortune of being permitted to live at this time,' he wrote later with unusual sincerity (*Mein Kampf*, 1939). By chance a photograph of the ecstatic crowd thronging the Odeonsplatz (a major square) in Munich on 2 August, captured Hitler, face lit up, exulting in the general patriotic fervour. The next day he petitioned King Ludwig III for permission to volunteer in the Bavarian army, although still an Austrian. (Bavaria remained a semi-autonomous kingdom within the federated German empire, like many small German states.) Amid the administrative chaos of the first days of the war, Hitler was granted his request. 'Within a few days I was wearing that uniform which I was not to put off again for nearly six years,' he said proudly (*Mein Kampf*, 1939).

The First World War *made* Adolf Hitler. It gave him a home, a sense of purpose and belonging and a guarantee of food and shelter – if often in a trench – for the first time since leaving Linz. Above all, its chaotic aftermath would allow the transformation of the aimless would-be artist into a demagogue of amazing power. But first Hitler was to fight right through over four years of war. He joined the List Regiment (named after its commander). The regiment soon saw heavy fighting in the First Battle of Ypres in Belgium against the British in November, losing three-quarters of its men before being pulled back. Hitler served throughout the war as a dispatch-runner (*Meldegänger*), carrying messages from the regimental command post to the front line often two miles away. He later gave the impression that he had actually served in the trenches, until political enemies revealed the truth, but he was in almost as much danger as if he had. In November he was promoted to Corporal and in December 1914 awarded the Iron Cross Second Class, which testified to his courage and competence. But he was never promoted to a higher rank of non-commissioned officer although this would have been expected for such a long-serving, keen soldier. Asked about this years later, his former officers said they considered him 'lacking in leadership potential'.

His fellow soldiers certainly found 'Adi', as they called him, odd. Instead of taking part in the usual jokes and grumbles about trench life, he sat quietly by himself, sometimes sketching or reading – Hitler later claimed to have read the entire works of the pessimistic philosopher Schopenhauer in the trenches – but more often lost in thought or daydreams. He never received any presents, even at Christmas, and few letters or cards, neither did he talk about his family or girlfriends, like other soldiers. When a telephonist one day suggested 'looking round for a Mamsell', Hitler exclaimed 'I'd die of shame looking for a French girl!' He showed affection only to a stray dog he called Foxl. Photographs show a gaunt face with staring eyes and a huge moustache. About the war itself he was deadly serious, disapproving of the spontaneous Christmas Truce of 1914, when British and German troops met in no man's land and sang carols together. Any discussion of the war, especially any pessimism as to its course, would rouse him to long speeches on how German victory was inevitable unless Germany's internal enemies, the Jews and Communists, destroyed it from within. His comrades found him uncongenial company and generally left him alone.

The List Regiment fought in the Battle of the Somme in 1916 and in October Hitler was wounded in the leg, being sent back to Germany to convalesce. There he saw Berlin for the first time, admiring its grandeur but dismayed at the civilian defeatism he found. He was keen to rejoin his regiment in March 1917, taking part in the last great German offensive in April 1918 which almost captured Paris. This was repulsed with heavy losses by the Allies, who then themselves attacked. On 4 August 1918 Hitler was awarded the Iron Cross First Class, very rarely given to corporals. (Ironically, the officer who recommended him, Hugo Gutman, was Jewish.) What Hitler won this for is uncertain – later Nazi tales describing him capturing 15 Frenchmen single-handed are implausible. He probably got it for delivering messages in unusually dangerous circumstances, but it helped his later career greatly. In October the List Regiment, under heavy pressure like the rest of the German army, suffered a gas attack near Ypres. Hitler and several comrades were partly blinded in it, and he was invalided back to Pomerania in north-east Germany. The war was over for him and very soon it was over for all Germany.

This was something that neither soldiers at the front nor civilians at home had been led to expect by the German high command, who had kept up confident talk of victory until the very end. In fact the German economy had been suffering slow strangulation from the British naval blockade for four years and the German 1918 offensive had been their last desperate attempt to break through before American troops began arriving in large numbers. (The USA entered the war in April 1917 almost without an army, creating one from scratch.) In October 1918 the new Prime Minister, Prince Max of Baden, had to tell the Reichstag the terrible truth: Germany faced imminent collapse, even mass starvation, and must sue for peace. This triggered a series of mutinies, riots and risings across Germany, leading to the flight of the Kaiser (Emperor) and all the lesser princes. In their place, amid defeat, chaos and national humiliation, the Weimar Republic was born – so-called because it had moved to the small city of Weimar for its inaugural meetings. Berlin at the time had become a battleground between the Spartacist Communists, intent on founding a Russian-style Soviet, and right-wing soldiers whom the Weimar politicians reluctantly called in to repress them.

Yet in November 1918 the German Imperial Army had still appeared to be unbeaten, for it occupied much of Russia – a country it had defeated – Belgium and northern France. In reality, it too was about to disintegrate. It had suffered almost seven million casualties (2.5 million dead) during the war – it had mobilized 10.5 million men out of Germany's population of 65 million – and was breaking down due to mass desertions and the influenza epidemic. Above all, the great Allied offensive which had begun in August was driving it back all along the front. However, German regiments, after the armistice of 11 November, were permitted to march back across the Rhine with banners flying, as if unbeaten. Thus grew up the myth of the 'Stab in the back': that Germany's armies, unconquered in the field, had been betrayed by 'traitors' at home, especially Jews and Communists.

Still half-blinded in hospital, Hitler heard the news of Germany's surrender with shocked disbelief. 'Everything went black before my eyes as I staggered back to my ward and buried my aching head between the blankets and pillow … And so it had all been in vain … Did all this happen only so that a gang of wretched criminals could get control of the fatherland? … The following days were terrible to bear and the nights still worse … In those nights my hatred increased, hatred for the originators of this crime.' (*Mein Kampf*, 1939) The crime was permitting Germany's surrender, which Hitler, along with millions of others, both soldiers and civilians, blamed on the new republic. At the time, however, Hitler was, unsure what to do with himself. With no home to go to, he wanted to stay in the army as long as possible, volunteering for guard duty near the Austrian border, and only reluctantly returning to Munich in February 1919.

He found it the centre of even more political violence than Berlin. The Wittelsbach monarchy had been thrown out in November and an unstable revolutionary coalition of Socialists, Marxists and Anarchists had taken its place, with 'Red Guards' tramping the corridors of palaces where powdered footmen had recently served royalty. Elections in

January reduced the radical USPD to a rump as Bavaria revealed its true conservative self, and a Social Democrat government took its place. But this could not control events either, and on 6 April a full 'Soviet Republic' was proclaimed by extremists in Munich. It lasted less than a month, ending in violence and bloodshed on both sides, as regular troops combined with many Freikorps – armed bands of ex-soldiers – to crush it. But it left a bitter legacy of distrust between left-wing groups, and paranoia about Marxism and Jews (several leaders of the Soviet had been Jewish) among the general public that undermined the Weimar Republic in Bavaria from its birth.

Exactly what role Hitler played in these stirring events is unclear. He glosses over them in just one page in *Mein Kampf* – a most unusual brevity – saying that he used his rifle to drive off three men sent by the Soviet to arrest him in April. His real role seems to have been far from heroic, and he probably accepted the Social Democrat government when it was in office. In May 1919 he attended a course of 'political instruction' for troops and was appointed an Instruction Officer himself in August, his first step on the political ladder. His chief role was to counter any Socialist or pacifist propaganda that could infect the troops, for which his habitual harangues made him well suited. His 'popular manner' and 'passionate fanaticism' were noted approvingly by his superiors. He was also used as an informer or spy to report on political developments in Munich. In such a role, on 12 September 1919 he was sent to a meeting of the DAP (*Deutsche Arbeiter-Partei*, German Workers' Party) in a Munich beerhall.

The DAP had been founded by a Bavarian locksmith, Anton Drexler, in January 1919. Its membership at the time was only about 40, mostly cranks and bores. Hitler was about to leave the meeting, bored himself, when a Professor Baumann extolled Bavarian independence, then a popular idea. Hitler intervened, attacking the proposal with such pan-Germanist fury that Baumann left the room. Impressed, Drexler gave Hitler some of his pamphlets, inviting him to return in a few days and join the movement. That night, Hitler read Drexler's propaganda, feeling a marked sympathy with its views. Going along a few days later to an obscure beerhall, he found the party's committee – Drexler and three other people – seated 'under the dim light shed by a grimy gas-lamp' (Hitler, Adolf *Mein Kampf*, 1939). Soon after, Hitler joined the party. He was not, as he claimed, its seventh member but he was certainly a very early one.

'Goodness, he's got the gift of the gab. We could use him,' Anton Drexler reputedly said after hearing Hitler speak that first night (Franz-Witling, Georg *Die Hitlerbwegung; Der Ursprung, 1919–22*, 1967). But it was Hitler who was to use the DAP on his road to power.

The making of a demagogue 3

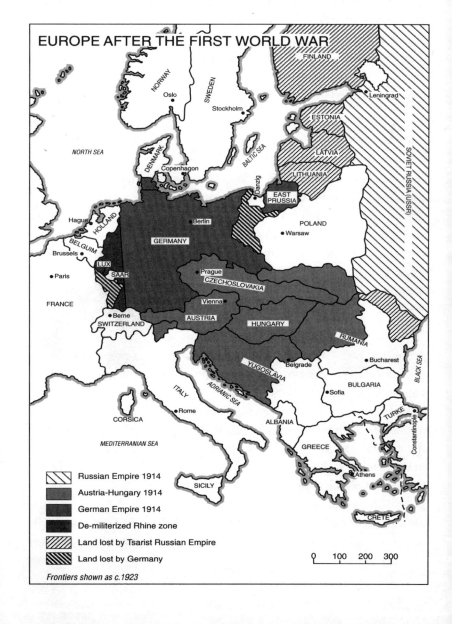

EUROPE AFTER THE FIRST WORLD WAR

NORWAY
Oslo

SWEDEN
Stockholm

FINLAND

Leningrad

NORTH SEA

DENMARK
Copenhagon

BALTIC SEA

ESTONIA

LATVIA

LITHUANIA

SOVIET RUSSIA (USSR)

Danzig

EAST
PRUSSIA

Hague
HOLLAND

Berlin

POLAND

Warsaw

BELGIUM
Brussels

GERMANY

LUX

Paris

SAAR

Prague
CZECHOSLOVAKIA

FRANCE

Vienna

Berne
SWITZERLAND

AUSTRIA

HUNGARY

RUMANIA

YUGOSLAVIA

Belgrade

Bucharest

BLACK SEA

ADRIATIC SEA

BULGARIA

Sofia

ITALY

Rome

CORSICA

ALBANIA

TURKE

Constantinople

MEDITERRANIAN SEA

GREECE

SICILY

Athens

CRETE

Russian Empire 1914

Austria-Hungary 1914

German Empire 1914

De-militerized Rhine zone

Land lost by Tsarist Russian Empire

Land lost by Germany

0   100   200   300

Frontiers shown as c.1923

The DAP (German Workers' Party) that Hitler joined in September 1919 was not an impressive organization. With only 40 members and 7.50 Marks in its bank account, it was typical of many tiny, extreme right-wing parties that had sprung up in Germany since the war. Drexler, who had founded it in January 1919, with glasses, meerschaum pipe and *Lederhosen* (leather shorts) looked like a schoolteacher, not a man of action. The DAP's very obscurity appealed to Hitler, however. In a large established party he would have been a nobody, but he could influence the DAP almost at its birth.

The new Weimar Republic which the DAP and other *völkisch* (nationalist populist) parties hated, has been called the 'Republic without Republicans', meaning that few Germans supported it. Its constitution was very democratic – it gave women the vote for the first time, granted states like Bavaria near-autonomy, guaranteed individual liberties and, through proportional representation, perfectly reflected votes. But democracy was not what many in crisis-ridden post-war Germany wanted. The Communists, following the official party line from Moscow, dismissed the Republic as 'bourgeois', refusing to co-operate with the larger Social Democrat party, which did support the Republic. But it was enemies on the right that presented the real danger.

At its inception the Republic left in place institutions which were fundamentally hostile to it, as were the people running them. Chief among these was the army, the glory of Prussia – in the eighteenth century the French philosopher Voltaire had joked that Prussia was not a state defended by an army but an army supported by a state. During the war, the military high command had exercised a near-dictatorship in Germany, but the army was reduced to a skeletal 100,000 men by the Treaty of Versailles, which the Weimar Republic reluctantly signed in June 1919. By this Germany also had to surrender all its battleships and airforce, its colonies in Africa and several provinces in Europe – chiefly Alsace-Lorraine, and, in the east, Posen and Danzig, which a newly independent Poland took. Most galling to German national pride were the articles of the Treaty admitting German war guilt – that Germany had started the war – and the demilitarization of the Rhineland.

From the start, the Republic's acceptance of the Versailles Treaty damned it not just with the army but with judges, police officers, teachers, academics – in fact most Germans. They could not accept that their cause in the war had not been just, and found Germany's post-war treatment outrageously unjust. The worsening economic situation also undermined parties supporting the Treaty, which lost seats in the Reichstag (national parliament) elections held in late June 1919. Some who rejected the Republic hoped for a return of Kaiser (Emperor) Wilhelm II, now exiled in Holland, but others looked for scapegoats and a saviour inside Germany. Hitler soon offered both.

Although in *Mein Kampf* Hitler exaggerated his immediate impact on the DAP, he undoubtedly transformed it from a timid discussion group into an aggressive, publicity-seeking party. He insisted on hiring a permanent office, with typewriter and telephone, both formerly lacking. He introduced soldiers from the barracks as members and began charging admission to meetings, something unheard of until then. Soon he was gaining far more attention with his growing rhetorical gifts than other fringe party speakers. At a meeting in October he attracted 111 listeners, rising to 200. In January 1920 Hitler took over the party's propaganda and on 24 February he advertised its first mass meeting in the Hofbräuhaus. Almost 2,000 people turned up to hear first the billed speaker, who failed to thrill, and then Hitler. He enthused the audience less with the party's 'Twenty-Five Point Programme' than by his ranting, hate-filled diatribes and the meeting ended in a near-riot, as was common at the time. The Hofbräuhaus meeting later was hailed as the true launch of the NSDAP (National Socialist German Workers' Party, shortened to Nazi), as it was renamed. Hitler helped design the distinctive Nazi flag – a black swastika in a white circle on a red ground. He finally knew that 'what before I had simply felt within me ... was now proved by reality: I could speak!' (*Mein Kampf*, 1939). Buoyed up by this discovery, he left the army in March 1920. He had at last found his true career and an outlet for all his resentments and fantasies.

Hitler used to speak from rough notes, often for two hours or more. He quickly learnt how to capture and excite his audience with rhetorical tricks. He developed these over the years, varying them according to his audience – for a gathering of great industrialists he adopted a more reasonable tone than with beerhall Brownshirts. Typically, he would arrive late, so that tension had already built up. He would start with low sarcastic comments and heavily rhetorical questions, his voice rising gradually to shouts and snarls of hate and triumph, while he made histrionic stabbing gestures, pushing back the hair from his forehead and stamping his feet as if on his enemies' head. Today such gestures may seem laughably clichéd (they inspired Charlie Chaplin in *The Great Dictator*) but they proved drastically effective at the time.

What Hitler actually *said* was seldom original, as he combined a ragbag of nationalistic and racist ideas and slogans taken from others. It was the conviction, vehemence and simplicity with which he proclaimed them, over and over again, that swayed his listeners and makes him perhaps the greatest demagogue in history. 'To be a leader means to be able to move masses,' he explained candidly in *Mein Kampf*. '...The masses are poorly acquainted with abstract ideas, their reactions lie more in the domain of feelings ... Whoever wishes to win over the masses must know the key to open the door to their hearts ... The masses' receptive powers are very restricted and their understanding feeble ... Effective propaganda must be confined to a few bare necessities expressed in a few stereotyped formulas.' Hitler became the master of such formulaic stereotyping.

Among Hitler's recurrent targets were the 'criminals of Versailles' – meaning the Allies, and even more the Weimar politicians who signed the Treaty – Jews, big business, war profiteers, Socialists, Communists, especially the allegedly 'Marxist' government in Berlin. To 'protect' the NSDAP gatherings from such groups, Hitler recruited a bodyguard of ex-soldiers which in 1921 became the *Sturmabteilung*, the SA or storm section, known as Brownshirts. As Hitler believed that attack was the best form of defence, Brownshirts began breaking up other parties' meetings as well as violently expelling hecklers from Nazi gatherings. In September 1921 he personally led a group to break up a meeting held by the Bavarian separatists, silencing their main speaker. In November the SA engaged in a near-battle with 'Reds' in the Saalschlacht (Hall Battle).

A year later Hitler took 800 uniformed Brownshirts to Coburg for a demonstration, fighting a pitched battle in its streets with Socialist and Communist opponents. Far from apologizing for his supporters' violence, Hitler exulted in it, realizing that spectators were as much thrilled as shocked. Thanks to Ernst Röhm, a heavy-drinking war veteran who had joined the party late in 1919 and had numerous contacts in the Bavarian police and the army, the Bavarian state generally turned a blind eye to Nazi thuggery. Conservative ministers in Bavaria's state government deplored Hitler's vulgarity but applauded his opinions and thought they could use him for their own ends – the first of many to make this terrible mistake.

By now Hitler was addressing Nazi meetings as the billed star speaker, attracting audiences exceeding 2,000. These consisted of white-collar workers, small tradesmen along with manual workers and even some women, all easily moved by Hitler's simplistic passions. 'He was at the time simply the greatest popular speaker without precedent,' said Hans Frank, later hanged for war crimes, recalling first hearing Hitler speak (Frank, Hans *Im Angesicht des Galgens*, 1953). In 1920, Hitler spoke at more than 30 meetings, and the party began to grow, from 190 members in January 1920 to 2,000 by December and 3,300 by August 1921. From the start the NSDAP was both nationalistic and egalitarian, even proletarian, unlike earlier nationalist parties which had appealed chiefly to the middle classes. The Twenty-Five Point Programme, which remained the only official programme, included radical measures such as closing down department stores, which threatened small shopkeepers, and expropriating land, but this 'socialism' was subordinate to virulent nationalism.

In December 1920, the party bought the bankrupt newspaper *Völkischer Beobachter* (People's Observer), with money lent by supporters such as Dietrich Eckart, a poet and journalist and the paper's first Nazi editor. The *Beobachter* became the Nazi mouthpiece, carrying frequent articles by Hitler – 39 in the first half of 1921 alone, probably providing his main source of income. (Exactly how Hitler lived in these years remains a mystery, but his lifestyle was hardly extravagant, for he occupied one squalid room. At this time he wore a cheap blue suit and shabby raincoat or trenchcoat but often spoke wearing a dark blue uniform, brandishing a whip.) His articles, like his speeches, were chiefly manic attacks with few positive proposals. But Hitler hardly needed concrete ideas. Events were playing into his hands.

In January 1921 at the Paris Conference the Western Allies demanded 226,000 million gold Marks from Germany in war reparations (the war in the west had been fought almost entirely in France and Belgium). Such a vast sum outraged all German political parties, further undermining the Republic. On 26 August 1921 the Reich Finance Minister Erzberger was murdered by a right-wing fanatic, a sign of growing anarchy. Walther Rathenau, Weimar's Foreign Minister who accepted the reparations demand, happened to be Jewish, more ammunition for nationalist opponents; he too was murdered in 1922. Even worse for Weimar was the Great Inflation which followed. The Reich Mark, which had stood at four to the US dollar in late 1918, began to fall, to 75 to the dollar by the summer of 1921, to 400 a year later and more than 7,000 by early 1923. By November 1923 it fell to 130,000 *million*, by which stage it was worthless. Inflation on such a scale affected every German, high and low, rich and poor, male and female. Although a tiny number profited, most saw their earnings and savings literally rendered valueless. Normal business became impossible as people had to carry bags full of banknotes around for any transaction. The search for scapegoats intensified.

Hitler had had to face down a threat from the committee led by Drexler to his growing dictatorship within the Nazi Party. This threat had arisen while Hitler was visiting Berlin in June 1921. Hurrying back to Munich, he countered accusations of a 'lust for power and personal ambition' by offering to resign. As Hitler by then *was* the Nazi Party, the committee capitulated, making him President with unlimited powers and retiring Drexler as 'Honorary President'. Hitler began moulding the party to fit his own ideas, introducing the raised arm 'Hitler salute' and the title *Führer* (leader) and encouraging the cult of leader. The Fascist leader (*duce*) Mussolini's 'March on Rome' in October 1922, which led to a Fascist *coup d'état*, proved a great inspiration.

Among new adherents to the Nazi cause was Hermann Göring, once commander of the famed Richthofen Fighter Squadron in the war, a bluff, brutish man with a rich and glamorous Swedish wife. Through Göring, Hitler met wealthy Nazi sympathizers such as the Bechstein family, the famous piano manufacturers. Hitler now began moving in much smarter Bavarian circles, where his mixture of 'Austrian' gentility – kissing his hostess's hand and giving her great bouquets of flowers – and aggressive rants against Jews and other enemies, in between wolfing down great quantities of cream cakes, struck an odd but unforgettable note. Soon money from such rich followers began flowing into Nazi coffers.

At the same time Hitler was strengthening links with the right-wingers in the Bavarian state government, who shared the Nazis' rejections of democracy and the Republic. In January 1923 the French army occupied the Rhineland and Ruhr, Germany's industrial heartland, to exact unpaid reparations in kind. This united all Germany again, although Hitler had no time for a national unity he could not use for his own purposes. Despite a fiasco on 1 May 1923, when a Nazi attempt to break up the traditional May Day parade by force was squashed by police, the Nazi movement was growing rapidly, as food riots broke out, trains and shops being raided by the almost starving populace. General Ludendorff, the supreme wartime hero, now began collaborating in right-wing plans to overthrow the Republic. He added vital prestige and respectability to the Nazis by joining Hitler on a political platform on 2 September 1923.

Although the Reichswehr (central army) remained loyal to the Republic, Bavarian troops and police under the state ministers Kahr, Seisser and Lossow were ambivalent about repressing the far right, dominated by Hitler. With the SA under Röhm numbering 15,000 armed men, Hitler began to plan a coup while circumstances and such ministers favoured him. He intended to use right-wingers in the Bavarian government for his own ends as they hoped to use him for theirs. On the evening of 8 November 1923, Göring burst into a political meeting attended by Kahr, Seisser and Lossow, followed by Hitler and many Brownshirts. Hitler leapt onto a chair, fired a revolver in the air and proclaimed: 'The National Revolution has begun! The hall is occupied by 600 armed men. No one may leave. The Bavarian and Reich governments have been removed and a provisional National government formed.' The last parts were bluff, but Hitler did have armed men at his command and the police had been persuaded not to intervene. Hitler told Kahr and his companions that he was forming a new government with Ludendorff as his Minister for War, and they must join it or die. When Ludendorff arrived, displeased at being told nothing beforehand and being expected to serve under Hitler, all three ministers reluctantly agreed to join, but being left unguarded they later managed to slip away and remove the Bavarian state government to Regensburg. The putsch was already going badly.

Next morning, as the SA set up machine-gun posts across Munich, Ludendorff persuaded Hitler that they must march on Lossow's headquarters, confident that soldiers would not fire on such a famous general. At the head of 3,000 storm troopers, Hitler and Ludendorff set out towards the main Odeonsplatz, but found their way blocked by armed police. Hitler cried out 'Surrender!' but in vain. Who fired first has never been established but bullets swept the street. Scheubner-Richter, who had been marching arm-in-arm with Hitler, was killed and fell to the ground, dragging Hitler down and dislocating his shoulder. Göring was badly wounded but Ludendorff, head held high, marched on unhurt and unchecked through the police cordon. Hitler fled back through the broken procession and escaped in a car, followed ignominiously by the other Nazi chiefs, abandoning their men. The attempted coup, ludicrously mismanaged, was over. Two days later Hitler was arrested in the house of Putzi Hanfstängel, a wealthy supporter, where he was being nursed.

Hitler later explained his failure as stemming from not winning over the army. 'We never thought to carry through a revolt against the Army: it was *with it* that we believed we should succeed.' (*Mein Kampf,* 1939) Even so, it was an achievement for someone who four years before had been a nobody to come so close to overthrowing the government. And Hitler was to use his forthcoming trial to maximum effect.

4 The rise to Chancellor

If the 'beerhall putsch', as the coup was soon called, proved a fiasco, with Hitler and other tough-talking Nazis fleeing at the first gunfire, Hitler brilliantly managed to turn his trial for treason to his own advantage, using the courtroom as a soapbox. The trial opened on 26 February 1924, lasting 24 days, and attracted the attention of the national and international press for the first time. As the chief witnesses for the prosecution – the officials Kahr, Lossow and Seisser – were almost as guilty of conspiring against the Republic as him, Hitler exploited their embarrassment, accusing them in court of having supported the attempted coup all along. The Minister of Justice Franz Gürtner was a Nazi sympathizer and the judges were easily swayed by Hitler's rhetoric. When Hitler declared, 'I alone bear the responsibility but I am not a criminal because of that … There is no such thing as treason against the traitors of 1918' [those who signed the Versailles Treaty], he was voicing the opinion of many Germans. One of the judges exclaimed, 'What a splendid fellow this Hitler is!' (Deuerlain, Ernst *Hitler's Entritt in die Politik und die Reichswehr*, 1959) The President of the Court only reprimanded those who applauded Hitler's long speeches too loudly.

Hitler's sentence – five years in Landsberg prison – was absurdly light, although he risked deportation after it (he was still officially Austrian). He was given a large airy room, where he received visitors bringing flowers and cakes, was allowed to hold court, with Nazi fellow-prisoners and even some wardens saluting him, and could stroll in the gardens, wearing Lederhosen, not prison uniform. He began dictating the first part of *Mein Kampf* (My Struggle), his weird hybrid of manifesto and autobiography, to the faithful Rudolf Hess, imprisoned with him. An almost unreadably turgid book, which sold in millions only after his rise to power, it reveals alarmingly Hitler's tortuous, paranoid half-educated mind – especially his obsessions with the Jews and Marxism and the need for Germany to expand east into Russia for its *Lebensraum* (living space), rather than south or overseas. This meant that Italy and Britain could become German allies, unlike in the First World War. Throughout the book Hitler reiterated his belief in struggle between the races as a central, desirable, part of history, with the 'Aryan' or Nordic races conquering other inferior peoples. 'Man has become great through struggle ... Whatever goal man has reached is connected with three concepts: struggle is the father of all things, virtue lies in blood, leadership is primary and decisive.' (Hitler, Adolf *Mein Kampf*, 1939) This 'Social Darwinism' was common at the time, but Hitler, adding a viciously racist twist, made it the key Nazi belief.

With its leader intent on his writing, the Nazi Party, officially banned, began to break up. Although the *völkisch* bloc of rightist parties did well in the April Bavarian elections, they did far worse in the national Reichstag elections at the end of the year. The Nazis especially seemed a write-off. Just after his arrest, Hitler had entrusted the leadership to Alfred Rosenberg, an introverted incapable mystic. Röhm founded the Frontbann as a successor to the SA, a paramilitary group whose rowdy independence soon annoyed Hitler and alarmed the Bavarian authorities. By the time Hitler was released on parole on 20 December 1924, after serving just ten months of his sentence, there was almost no Nazi Party left. Probably this was what he intended: better the party should be eclipsed than be led by someone else.

Hitler had announced in prison that, 'instead of trying to win power by force, we must hold our noses and enter the Reichstag against the Catholic and Marxist deputies ... Sooner or later we shall have a majority' (Deuerlain, Ernst, 1959). He began rebuilding his position within the party and in Germany. He called on the President of Bavaria, Dr Held, on 4 January, promising that in future the Nazis would respect the law – a promise he more or less kept until he became Chancellor. The ban on the party and its newspaper was lifted, Held complacently telling Gürtner, 'The wild beast is checked. We can afford to loosen the chain.' In one way Held was right: the ranting putschist was now overlaid or disguised by the wily politician, scheming rather than shooting his way to the top.

On 27 February 1925 Hitler relaunched the party with a rally in the Bürgerbräukeller for 4,000 of the faithful, whom he galvanized again with his rhetoric – too successfully, for he was then banned from speaking in public in Bavaria and most German states, a big setback for such a fiery orator. An even bigger setback was Germany's economic and political recovery in the mid-1920s. Dr Schacht, called in to rescue the German currency, had introduced the Rentenmark, based on property, and ended inflation in early 1924. The Dawes Plan renegotiated German reparation payments, the French army evacuated the Ruhr, the Locarno Pact guaranteed Germany's frontiers in the west and in September 1926 Germany became a member of the League of Nations, the forerunner of the UN from which it had initially been excluded. Germany under the Republic seemed to be recovering its international position peacefully, while the economy, fuelled by American loans, boomed. By 1927 German industrial production had reached 122 per cent of its 1913 figure, having sunk to 55 per cent in 1923, and unemployment fell to 650,000. This was the Weimar Republic's brief Golden Age, when its cinema, architecture and literature made Berlin one of the world's greatest cities. Hitler had no time for this decadent 'Jewish–Marxist' art.

In March 1925 the völkisch parties, including the Nazis, supported Ludendorff as their candidate for the presidential elections (the president was the Republic's umpire, the chancellor its prime minister). Ludendorff gained only 211,000 votes out of 27 million and the Nazis supported the aged Field-Marshal von Hindenburg in the second round, so alienating Ludendorff, who became increasingly eccentric. The victory of Hindenburg, while dismaying some democrats, paradoxically strengthened the Republic by reconciling many conservatives to it – for the time being. Its strength was shown by the rout of the anti-democrats in the Reichstag elections of May 1928, when the Nazis won only 12 seats.

Despite these unfavourable circumstances, the Nazi Party continued to recruit fee-paying members, numbers steadily increasing from 27,000 in 1925 (though few of these were in Munich), to 178,000 in 1929. This increase enabled salaried *Gauleiters* (district leaders) to be appointed around Germany to organize the party nationally. It also allowed Hitler to live partly off expenses, for he still made only modest amounts from his writings. For 20,000 marks he now bought a large turbo-charged Mercedes, in which he loved being driven around at high speed – he never learnt to drive – and began renting a villa, Haus Wachenfeld, in the Alps at Obersalzberg at 100 Marks a month. Later he bought this and enlarged it into the Berghof, his notorious mountain retreat. It was in this part of the world that he felt most at home, but in 1929 he also started renting a fine nine-bedroomed apartment in a smart area of Munich. He later described these days in Munich as the happiest of his life, spending long periods at Obersalzberg, going on picnics with a few cronies and his then girlfriend Geli (see p. 52). A more elevated recreation was his frequent visits to the opera, especially to hear Wagner's operas at Bayreuth. Introduced to the heirs of Richard Wagner, he paid homage to the dead master's memory and won over Wagner's heirs, important figures, to Nazism.

Crucially, in the mid-1920s Hitler strengthened his position vis-à-vis the party and its members. The brothers Gregor and Otto Strasser had emerged as leading Nazis in northern Germany, with their own Berlin newspaper. Gregor Strasser was a Reichstag deputy, and he travelled round Germany meeting Gauleiters. Josef Goebbels, a young Rhinelander with a higher degree – common in Germany but not among the ill-educated Nazis – became the Strassers' very competent secretary. The northern Nazis were genuinely Socialist in some ways, especially in their beliefs that the former German princes' property should be expropriated and that Soviet Russia was a potential Nazi ally.

They often criticized Hitler and the Munich party in general. As Hitler was trying, with limited success, to get support from rich German industrialists and was already receiving a subsidy from a princess, such ideas were anathema to him. Even worse was their indirect challenge to his leadership.

In February 1926 he summoned a meeting of all Nazis at Bamberg, in northern Bavaria, arriving in his Mercedes escorted by many Brownshirts. Using all his charm and oratory, he won over Goebbels who became his devoted follower and the Strassers' bitter enemy. The row with the northern Nazis was patched up, and in July Hitler held a rally of 5,000 Nazis at Weimar in Thuringia, one of the few states where he was allowed to speak. The next year, after the ban on his speaking in Bavaria was lifted, he spoke at a bigger rally in Nuremberg, from then on the great centre of Nazi rallies. These became scenes of mass intoxication with Hitler's rhetoric, a moment when the whole party renewed its devotion to the Führer.

In November 1926 Hitler made Goebbels gauleiter of 'Red' (Communist) Berlin, a difficult posting which he filled brilliantly, building up the Nazi movement there and countering the Strassers' power in the north. In November 1928 Hitler appointed Goebbels Nazi Propaganda Chief. He was to become one of the greatest propagandists of all time. Göring, now returned from exile, was also living in Berlin, moving in upper-class circles which proved useful politically. With Goebbels he was one of the 12 Nazi deputies elected in 1928. Meanwhile Hitler again had problems with the refounded SA – Röhm had gone off to Bolivia annoyed by Hitler's restrictions on it – which constantly degenerated into a boozy, brawling mob. He finally made himself head of it, but began creating his own highly disciplined bodyguard, which became the SS (*Schutz Staffeln*, protection guard) under Heinrich Himmler in 1929. That same year the Brown House, an impressive building in Munich, became the Nazi headquarters.

All this must have struck observers as irrelevant as long as Weimar's good times lasted. But in October 1929 Wall Street, the US stock market, crashed, ushering in the Great Depression. Germany was acutely vulnerable as it depended on short-term American loans. As these were called in, the German economy plunged. Unemployment climbed to three million in September 1930 and to six million early in 1932, or over 20 per cent. This set off a vicious circle, for unemployment relief was funded by national insurance, whose revenues fell as the numbers in work declined. 'I lost all I possessed through adverse economic conditions, so early in 1930 I joined the Nazi Party,' said one unskilled labourer, voicing working-class despair (Abel, Theodor *Why Hitler Came to Power*, 1938). The middle classes, still scarred by inflation, felt the ill effects just as badly, for they risked losing their respectability and falling into the ranks of the proletariat from which many had only recently climbed. Simplistic solutions and scapegoats – the French, the Jews, Communists, speculators – offered by the Nazis were once more welcome as Goebbels revived old popular hatreds.

The always frail Republic's demise was now made inevitable by the myopic arrogance of its leading politicians. In March 1930 the fragile centre-left coalition broke up – a problem with the Republic was that too many tiny parties were represented in the Reichstag due to proportional representation – and Heinrich Brüning of the Catholic Centre Party became Chancellor of a minority government. His obvious allies were the right-wing Nationalists, led by Alfred Hugenberg, with one-sixth of the seats, but Hugenberg refused to co-operate. Brüning began governing by emergency decree, Article 48 of the Constitution, which President Hindenburg authorized, then in September 1930 he called an election. To everyone's amazement, the Nazis won 107 seats, gaining chiefly in the deeply conservative north German countryside and small towns, which they had been wooing with promises of food tariffs to protect agriculture. Their support came partly from former Nationalists but many across the political spectrum now looked to Hitler as a possible saviour. However, the

Communists also gained seats, and on the streets clashes between the unleashed SA and Communists grew ever more violent. Normal life seemed to be breaking down.

In late 1930 Brüning tried to lure Hitler into joining the government with a cabinet post, but Hitler refused to participate in any government dependent on Socialists. Brüning continued without a Reichstag majority, indeed increasingly without using the Reichstag at all, relying instead on emergency decrees. Brüning's economic policy, like that of many leaders around the world at the time, consisted of retrenchment. Civil servants' salaries were cut by 40 per cent, unemployment benefits reduced, interest rates raised – all making the slump worse. Sickening of this, a group of businessmen and great landowners approached Hitler in the autumn of 1931 offering him a government post, but not as Chancellor. They intended to use the Nazis against the Communists and Socialists. Again Hitler refused. Early in 1932 Brüning tried to outwit Hitler by proposing that Hindenburg's term as President should be prolonged without the legally required election. Hitler, although reluctant to oppose the national hero, refused and decided to stand as president. Despite hectic campaigning, travelling around Germany by air, he lost, but he won an impressive third of the vote in April's second round election.

Soon after this Brüning was dismissed by Hindenburg, and Franz von Papen, a smooth but rather lightweight diplomat, became Chancellor. Real power, however, was held by Kurt von Schleicher, Defence Minister, in a 'Cabinet of Barons', solely representing great landowners and industrialists. Fresh Reichstag elections in July 1932 saw the Nazis win 230 seats or 37.6 per cent of the vote, making them much the largest party, and Göring accordingly became President of the Reichstag. In August power seemed in Hitler's grasp but all he was offered was the Vice-Chancellorship. This was not enough for him and negotiations collapsed. A vote of censure on von Papen passed by 512 votes to 42 on 12 September, but was technically invalid, as von Papen had just dissolved the Reichstag. In fresh elections in November the Nazi vote fell to 196 seats, but they were still the biggest party. The Communists, however, gained, winning 100 seats.

At this stage Hitler faced a crisis. Non-stop electioneering – for state as well as national elections – had emptied Nazi coffers completely. The Brownshirts, unpaid, were on the verge of mutiny, despite Röhm's reappointment as leader in 1931. Suddenly in December Schleicher offered the Vice-Chancellorship to Gregor Strasser, the eloquent 'left-wing' Nazi – with the double aim of splitting the Nazis and getting Schleicher made Chancellor. Schleicher indeed became Chancellor, the last Weimar Chancellor, but Strasser refused the offer. Instead, he attacked Hitler for betraying the movement before suddenly resigning. His position had been undermined by Hitler's subtle manoeuvrings and brilliant speech before the Nazi deputies. Von Papen, alarmed at the prospect of a leftist government, furtively approached Hitler, offering the Nazis financial support from bankers and industrialists. With Hindenburg's consent, von Papen also offered Hitler the Chancellorship, with himself as Vice-Chancellor and eight of the 11 other cabinet posts going to non-Nazis to keep the Nazis in check. Hitler now accepted, merely insisting that Göring should be Minister of the Interior in Prussia, the main state, and Frick, another Nazi, should be Reich Interior Minister. On 30 January 1933 Hindenburg finally appointed Hitler Chancellor. The 'national revolution' to create the Third Reich had begun, though few non-Nazis even in Germany as yet realized it.

5 The legal revolution

Tens of thousands of Brownshirts marched in torch-lit triumph through Berlin on 30 January 1933, the night Hitler became Chancellor, saluting their Führer now at last in power. Hitler had gained power not by force or by winning a popular majority as he had hoped, but by the political machinations he had long denounced. But he now proceeded, with astonishing speed and ease, to demolish the Weimar Republic and replace it with the Third Reich in what was, superficially, a legal revolution. (The Hohenzollern Kaisers' *Reich* or Empire of 1871–1918 had been the second Reich, the medieval Holy Roman Empire the first.)

Although von Papen had assured Hindenburg that Hitler and the Nazis would be tamed by being outnumbered in the Cabinet and by Hugenberg's Nationalists in the Reichstag, Hitler rapidly revealed his domination of the government. For the government to have a Reichstag majority, the Central Party needed to join the coalition, but Hitler sabotaged negotiations with them, making another election inevitable. This time, the Nazis controlled and unscrupulously used the radio (there was no television), and pressed big business into contributing generously to their funds. The Brownshirts went on the rampage, beating up opponents, smashing their offices, tearing down their posters, while the police turned a blind eye. Göring, as Interior Minister of Prussia, the largest state, had 'Nazified' the police by drafting 50,000 SA and SS men into the force, dismissing unco-operative civil servants. Goebbels began preparing for the biggest electoral campaign ever. Then the Nazis had a stroke of luck.

On the night of 27 February the Reichstag building mysteriously went up in flames. A mentally disturbed Dutchman with Communist sympathies, Marinus van der Lubbe, was arrested, apparently in the act, and confessed to setting fire to it as a protest. The Nazis claimed it was part of a Communist conspiracy and the next day an emergency degree proclaimed martial law, abolishing personal liberties. The truth about the Reichstag fire – whether it was started by the Nazis or by van der Lubbe acting on his own – remains unknown, but it certainly boosted the Nazis' campaign. Even so, despite massive demonstrations throughout Germany, with marches, rallies and open SA brutality, the Nazis won only 43.9 per cent of the vote in Germany's last free election. With the Nationalists, they now barely had a majority in the Reichstag, but soon they did not need even that.

On 21 March Hitler set out to win over the military by a special ceremony at Potsdam, the small town that Frederick the Great, Prussia's most famous king, had made synonymous with Prussia's military glory. All the marshals and generals of the First World War were there along with the crown prince, the swastika flag flew side by side with the red-white-black of the old imperial flag, Brownshirts faced soldiers, while Hitler, looking awkward in a tail coat, walked modestly behind Field-Marshal Hindenburg, resplendently uniformed. Hindenburg saluted the empty throne where once the Kaiser had sat, and read a brief speech. Hitler responded with similar appeals for national unity, then crossed to the old Marshal's chair, bowing low to grasp his hand as the camera bulbs flashed. This brilliant piece of political theatre reassured conservatives and Nationalists, especially in the army, that, despite continuing Nazi thuggery, Hitler himself could be trusted to restore Germany's military honour, prostrate since 1918.

The true spirit of the new Reich was shown two days later in the Reichstag. An Enabling Bill, effectively making the Reichstag irrelevant to government by giving the government full-time emergency powers, was brought before a house lined with armed SA and SS men; most of the 81 Communist and several liberal and SDP deputies had already been arrested. The Social Democrat leader made a brave plea for tolerance and liberty, provoking a vicious personal attack by Hitler – 'The star of Germany is in the ascendant, yours is about to disappear, your death-knell has sounded!' (Bullock, Alan *Hitler, A Study in Tyranny*, 1962) –

and the Reichstag passed the bill by 441 votes to 94. Outside crowds cheered the death of German democracy. The parliament of the most powerful country in Europe was now just a rubber stamp for a dictator.

Germany's federal structure, a potential obstacle to the *Gleichschaltung* (co-ordination) of full Nazi power, was also soon dismantled. On 9 March a *coup d'état* in Bavaria led to a Nazi takeover; Prussia was already Nazi-ruled and other states such as Baden and Saxony soon had Nazi state governments. On 31 March the diets (parliaments) of all states were dissolved. Soon after, Reich governors were appointed directly from Berlin. Soon the Nazi swastika had replaced the Republic's red, black and yellow flag in official buildings, symbolizing the dominance of the Nazi Party over local or state officials. The proud tradition of German federalism was at an end.

The huge trade union movement, which had often challenged governments in both the empire and the Republic, succumbed just as quickly. On May Day Hitler addressed a vast workers' rally in Berlin. Floodlit on a grandstand above the million-strong crowd, he received a rapturous ovation. As night fell he spoke in almost religious terms of the national renewal transcending all divisions. The very next day trade union offices across Germany were occupied, trade union officials being arrested and thrown into concentration camps, the unions dissolved and replaced by the Nazi Labour Front. Rival political parties were also soon extinguished. On 10 May Brownshirts occupied the Social Democrats' offices and their newspapers and funds seized, effectively marking the party's end. The many smaller parties were closed in June, Hugenberg's Nationalists, Hitler's supposed coalition allies, being suppressed on 28 June. On 14 July a new law simply banned all parties other than the Nazis. President Hindenburg, now very old but generally pleased with Hitler's progress, saw his dynamic Chancellor less and less. Even Hitler was surprised by his opponents' lack of resistance. 'One would never have thought so miserable a collapse possible,' he said in July (*The Ribbentrop Memoirs*, 1954). But the Republic's roots had been shallow from the start.

The Third Reich was from its start a police state. The rapid increase in the number of prisoners – by the end of March alone there were 100,000 more – led to the building of 'concentration camps', prison camps with barbed wire fences, outside cities at places like Buchenwald or Dachau. These were at first run by the SA and, although appallingly brutal, with prisoners regularly beaten to death, they were not as yet extermination camps. Most Germans, seeing Communists, Socialists, liberals, democrats, homosexuals, Jews and other 'national enemies' being rounded up and deported there – without any trial – were not unduly distressed, as they thought it could never happen to them. The regime took care to make it clear what would happen to those who stepped out of line, but the casual violence of the SA impressed, even attracted, more than it repelled. Göring developed a section of the Prussian police into the *Geheime Staatspolizei* (Secret State Police) or Gestapo, which soon covered all Germany. In 1934 Himmler, the quietly efficient head of the SS which already numbered 50,000, took over the Gestapo and began to build it, together with the SS, into a state within a state, a form of empire-building characteristic of Nazi Germany. By 1944 Himmler controlled a force of two million men.

The Nazis also had to come to terms with the Church, for Germany was nominally a Christian country, one-third Catholic. The Protestant churches had long been used to accepting state guidance, and most pastors accepted the Nazis initially. A 'Reich bishop' Ludwig Müller was appointed to Nazify Protestantism. Proclaiming that Christ was not really Jewish but a blond 'Aryan', he soon made himself ridiculous. Hitler, one of the most lapsed Catholics ever, despised all Protestants but retained some respect for the powers of the Catholic hierarchy. In July 1933 a Concordat was signed between Reich and Vatican, each promising to respect the other's sphere. 'What the old parliament and parties did not accomplish in 60 years, your statesmanship has achieved in six months' gushed Cardinal von Fauhalber to Hitler soon afterwards (Kupper, Alfons *Staatlike Akten über die Reichskonkordatsverhandlung*, 1969). Frictions later arose as the essentially anti-Christian nature of

Nazism became apparent but the Catholic Church as a body did little effective to oppose Nazism either in Germany or later across Europe.

Relations between the army and the SA were Hitler's biggest immediate problems. Hitler had won over the generals with his Potsdam ceremony and his secret plans to expand the army vastly – way beyond the 100,000 limit laid down by the Versailles Treaty – but such rearmament would need time. After 15 years' disarmament, Germany could not rapidly recreate the old imperial army, once the strongest in the world, although it was still the world's second greatest industrial power (after the USA), with brilliant engineering, electrical and chemical industries. Hitler also looked ahead to Hindenburg's death, when he would need army support for his own succession plans.

Meanwhile the Brownshirts, now numbering 2.5 million (against the army's 100,000), clamoured for recognition and reward. The 'Old Comrades', street fighters who had joined before the election victory of March 1933, demanded cushy jobs and perks, such as a Mercedes and an expense account. Although many offices did go to laughably incompetent Nazis, Hitler had no intention of wrecking the entire state by handing over key posts to boozy brawlers who beat up and imprisoned whomever they chose, sometimes picking on 'important' people. Neither would he accept the SA's radical economic demands for nationalizing land, abolishing unearned income and cutting interest rates. Above all, Hitler rejected Röhm's demand that the SA should form the basis for a new popular army, using the old Reichswehr simply to train this huge force under Röhm's command. Hitler himself despised the military aristocracy but, for the present, was prepared to use and flatter them. Throughout his early years as dictator, Hitler repeatedly displayed a cool-blooded calculation which kept potential opponents guessing, both at home and abroad.

All this delay aggravated the Brownshirts' and especially Röhm's resentment, for he alone among leading Nazis had no important post. Hitler, often surprisingly loyal to old comrades of the Munich days, at first tried reconciliation. In December 1933 he made Röhm Minister without Portfolio and a member of the Cabinet, and in the New Year wrote him a friendly letter recalling their joint struggles. In February 1934 a law gave Brownshirts injured in street fighting the same privileges and pensions as war veterans. This did not satisfy Röhm, however, who continued to press for a new ministry giving him control of the army. This alarmed all the army chiefs, who appealed to Hindenburg. In April Hitler assured the generals that he would rein in the SA, in return for their own support, but still he hesitated to act. Meanwhile the other leading Nazis, including Göring, Hess and Himmler – theoretically Röhm's subordinate as the SS was officially part of the SA – collected damning if often misleading information about Röhm's corruption, debauchery and, far worse, disloyalty. Certainly Röhm was privately critical of Hitler.

At the beginning of June 1934 Röhm met Hitler for a long talk. They agreed on nothing but Röhm accepted his orders that the whole SA should go on leave for July. He himself went off for a rest-cure at Wiessee in Bavaria. On 17 June von Papen, no longer an important figure but still Vice-Chancellor, made a speech at Marburg University attacking the prevalent 'confusion of brutality and vitality', saying 'No nation can live in a condition of permanent revolution from below.' (Jacobsen, Hans-Adolf and Werner, Jockmann *Ausgewhelte Dokumente*, 1961). Although Goebbels tried to hush up this speech, Hitler, fed with false reports that the SA were preparing for a coup, decided he must act if he were to retain the army's loyalty. On 25 June General von Fritsch, the Army Commander in Chief, placed the army on full alert. On the night of the 29th, Hitler flew to Munich. Very early on 30 June, picked forces of SS men burst into the hotel where Röhm was asleep and dragged him and many other Brownshirts, some sharing a bed, away to be summarily shot. Röhm's demands to be killed by Hitler himself were contemptuously ignored as two SS men emptied their revolvers into his naked body. Similar murders took place at the same time throughout Germany. Many of the arrested SA men died shouting 'Heil Hitler', so little did they understand what was happening.

In this 'Night of the Long Knives', at least 400 people, probably far more, were killed. These were mostly leading Brownshirts but some, like Gregor Strasser and Schleicher were not connected with the SA at all. Von Papen himself only just escaped with his life, his two advisors being shot dead. It was an occasion for settling old scores bloodily, not for careful justice, a concept alien to Nazism. There had almost certainly been no coup planned against the government that June, but the SA was an embarrassment to Hitler's attempts to become Hindenburg's successor. The generals were much relieved by events, Hindenburg thanking Hitler for 'his determined action and gallant intervention to nip treason in the bud'. Hitler himself, perturbed by this murder of old comrades, suffered bad stomach cramps. Justifying himself in the Reichstag on 13 July, he stressed the corruption, favouritism and perversion of Röhm's circle. 'It has been terribly hard for me to part with comrades who fought for years alongside me,' he said, but added, 'I gave the order to shoot those most guilty of treason ... For us there is no permanent revolution ... the fighting organizations of the Party are political institutions and have nothing to do with the Army.' (Domarus, Max *Der Reichstag und die Macht*, 1968). The SA now sank to a secondary role; in its place the SS began to grow.

On 2 August 1934, Hindenburg, father figure of the country, died. Within an hour it was announced that the office of President would be merged with that of Chancellor, Hitler taking both. He would thus become Head of State and Supreme Commander in Chief of the Armed Forces. That same day all officers and men in the army were required to swear a new oath of allegiance to Hitler personally: 'I swear by God ... I will render unconditional obedience to the Führer of the German Reich and People, Adolf Hitler.' On 19 August the Germans expressed in a plebiscite their approval of the new set-up, 89.93 per cent voting for it. At the Nuremberg rally in September Hitler announced an end to revolutionary turmoil. 'Revolutions have always been rare in Germany ... In the next thousand years there will be no other revolution in Germany.' His was to be the Thousand Year Reich.

Rebuilding Germany 6

Hitler, on coming to power, found Germany demoralized and weak both internally – due to the Great Depression, which had hit its economy even worse than most Western countries' – and vis-à-vis neighbouring nations, which almost all had far bigger armies. Dealing with Germany's massive unemployment was his most pressing priority domestically, but re-establishing Germany's armed strength was his overriding aim. Fortunately for him, the two could be tackled simultaneously, for rearmament stimulated employment.

Hitler knew nothing of economics but regarded political will as more important than economic science. In the spring of 1933 he appointed Dr Hjalmar Schacht, long a Nazi sympathizer, to head the Reichsbank (central bank) and, in 1934, the whole economy. Schacht proved a financial wizard, issuing 'Mefo-bills' of credit backed by hypothetical future tax revenues, to order goods and raw materials both at home and abroad long before the industries or ministries concerned could pay for them. Schacht managed to persuade the small countries in south-eastern Europe – Romania, Yugoslavia and Bulgaria, traditionally in the German economic sphere – to accept Mefo-bills and supply oil and food supplies merely for the promise of machinery or other goods. By the summer of 1939, the Germans were taking almost all the oil from Romania, the largest producer in Europe.

An expansive programme of public works, from massive sports stadia to land-reclamation schemes, led the German economy to recover remarkably quickly. Unemployment fell from almost six million in January 1933 to 2.6 million by December 1934. By 1936 there were shortages of skilled labour, by 1939 of almost all labour. Real wages recovered from their 1931 depths and had increased by 7 per cent above their 1928 levels by 1937. If they hardly increased after that, few Germans noticed in the general sense of restored national vigour.

The most obvious and glamorous of the Nazis' public works were the *Autobahn*s (motorways). Hitler inaugurated the construction of the first Autobahn in September 1933 with a tremendous fanfare, repeated over the years with further schemes. Six years later, when war broke out, the Autobahn network covered about 3,000 km (1,800 miles). By 1938 Autobahn construction was employing some 200,000 people directly. This was the first major motorway system in Europe (Mussolini had begun a modest Italian scheme earlier), and it encouraged a correspondingly rapid expansion of the German motor industry. This was an industry dear to Hitler's heart. He had appeared unexpectedly at the Berlin International Auto Festival in February 1933 to praise the auto industry as an 'industry of the future', and promised tax concessions to encourage it. Car production indeed surged, from 70,000 in 1931 to 340,000 in 1938, the last full year of peace. The *Beobachte*r, seeing a propaganda opportunity, promised Germans a 'Volkswagen' or People's Car, which every German worker would one day be able to afford by saving just 5 Marks a month. In practice, very few classic 'Beetles' were produced before war switched factory production to military vehicles. But the knock-on effects of this expansion stimulated all manufacturing, as did the general recovery in national self-confidence.

Coupled with this expansion went a programme of import-substitution wherever possible – and sometimes where not really desirable. For example, Germans wishing to buy one foreign orange might have to buy a whole kilo of German apples at the same time, whether they wanted the apples or not. This supported German agriculture at the expense of the urban consumer, but there were intermittent food shortages. Germany was never self-sufficient in food, as foreign currency, which went firstly to buying materials for the arms industries, was always in short supply. Very tight restrictions were imposed on the amount of currency travellers could take abroad. This had the added benefit, for the Nazis, of depriving exiles fleeing the new regime from taking more than a suitcase of belongings with them.

What they left behind was seized and handed over to Nazi chiefs. Other countries, principally the USA under Roosevelt's New Deal, pursued similar courses of public works with similar success, and economic recovery in Germany may have already just begun in 1933, but Hitler undoubtedly accelerated it. The conquest of unemployment was one of the Reich's proudest boasts – the Nazis crowed jubilantly when American unemployment figures climbed again briefly in 1937.

There was, however, one huge difference between Hitler's policies and those in America or elsewhere: the immensely ambitious rearmament programme Hitler wanted to implement as fast as possible. This was an essential to back up his ambitious and increasingly aggressive foreign policy. (The Autobahns, contrary to popular belief, had no real military purpose, as the Wehrmacht always relied on the railways for transporting its mostly unmotorized divisions. However, some Autobahn tunnels and bridges did serve as shelters for bombed out factories in the last stages of the war; by that time there was no petrol for cars.) Schacht stated in a secret memorandum in May 1935 that 'achieving the armament programme with speed and in quantity is *the* problem in German politics and everything else should be subordinated to this purpose as long as it is not imperilled by neglecting all other questions.' But at first rearmament proceeded covertly and fairly slowly, as the arms budgets reveal: 1.9 billion Marks were spent on arms in 1933–4 and the same in 1934-5. This climbed to 4 billion Marks in 1935–6, 5.8 billion in 1936–7, 8.2 billion in 1937-8 and 18.4 billion in 1938–9. By that time armaments consumed almost two-thirds of the entire budget, although Germany was still at peace.

Any expansion of Germany's armed forces broke the terms of the Versailles Treaty. However, Hitler proved masterly at confusing and dividing his opponents abroad, trading on feelings, especially in Britain, that Germany had been maltreated after 1918 and that some adjustment to the post-war settlement was overdue. On 17 May 1933, while a Disarmament Conference was in progress at Geneva, Hitler declared that, as Germany was the one country which had already disarmed, other countries must now do so or be seen as potential aggressors. 'It is in everyone's interests that today's problems be solved reasonably and peacefully,' he said, adding, 'Germany, in demanding equal rights that can only be attained by other nations disarming, has a moral right to do so, since she has herself fulfilled the requirements of the Treaty ... We have no greater wish than to contribute to finally healing the wounds caused by the War and the Treaty of Versailles.' The French, however – who then had the biggest if hardly the best army in Europe – had no intention of disarming, as Hitler well knew.

On 14 October 1933 Hitler proclaimed that Germany, for so long denied equal rights by the victors of the First World War, was withdrawing both from the Disarmament Conference and the League of Nations. 'The aim of the Versailles Treaty seems to be not to give humanity peace but rather to keep it in a state of unending hatred,' he said in justification. Withdrawing unilaterally from the League was a gamble by Hitler – the first of many – but it paid off, especially when a German referendum in November approved his policy by 95 per cent, giving his action democratic backing. One of the loathed 'shackles' of Versailles had been struck off.

Hitler could now claim that total disarmament was out of the question. All that could be discussed was agreeing to arms limits, and Germany's right to an army of 300,000 men (three times larger than the Weimar army) must be accepted as the starting point. In January 1934 Hitler surprised the world by signing a Ten-Year Non-Aggression Pact with Poland. Poland was traditionally despised by Germans and had a large German minority living in lands gained by it in 1918/19, but he needed to isolate Poland from France, its traditional ally. This foreign policy triumph was balanced by a fiasco in Austria, however. Hitler wanted to incorporate Austria into *Gross Deutschland* (Greater Germany) and when on 25 July 1934 Austrian Nazis murdered the Austrian Chancellor Dollfuss in a coup, he at first welcomed the news. But the coup soon collapsed and other powers reacted strongly. In particular Mussolini, the Italian dictator whom Hitler had visited but not impressed in April, ordered Italian tanks to the Brenner Pass on the frontier. The Germans had to disassociate themselves and return Dollfuss's murderers to Austria. With his rearmament programme only beginning, Hitler needed to tread carefully, talking the language of peace while covertly building up his forces. Germany in these first years of his rule was still extremely vulnerable, unarmed but still distrusted by its neighbours.

In January 1935 a plebiscite in the Saarland, the small, coal-rich territory on the French border detached in 1918, voted overwhelmingly for rejoining Germany. Hitler claimed that Germany did not wish to regain Alsace-Lorraine, the disputed French provinces occupied by it from 1871 to 1918, however. On 12 March 1935 the French government doubled the conscription period for French army recruits, solely to make up for the nation's falling birthrate. Hitler found this the perfect excuse for reintroducing conscription in Germany, aiming to create an army of 36 divisions or 540,000 men but calling it a defensive move against 'French militarism'. The Germans again applauded their Führer's determination to restore national pride. The French protested to the League at this further violation of the Versailles Treaty but did nothing. The British merely enquired if Hitler would still see Sir John Simon, the Foreign Secretary then visiting Berlin. Hitler did, boasting untruthfully that Germany had already achieved parity in air power with Britain – but here scoring an own goal, because the news spurred the pacific British Prime Minister Baldwin to double spending on the RAF. On 21 May Hitler secretly gave Schacht control of economic preparations for total war while making himself Supreme Commander of the Wehrmacht (army), but that same evening he made a long speech in the Reichstag denouncing the horrors of war.

This apparently peace-loving speech went down well in Britain, a country Hitler determined to woo. In *Mein Kampf* he had criticized the Kaiser's Germany for making enemies of both Britain and Russia. 'No sacrifice should have been thought too great to gain England's friendship. Colonial and naval ambitions should have been abandoned.' Leaving Britain to rule the waves, Germany should look east to the Russian plains for its empire. Some British Conservatives half-accepted this idea, seeing Nazi Germany as a bulwark against Soviet Russia. In June 1935 an agreement was signed between the two countries limiting Germany's navy to 35 per cent of Britain's, except for submarines, where it would have parity. 'Politically, I see the future only in alliance with the British,' declared Hitler, probably half-believing it. But, as Germany scarcely had any navy at the time, the treaty gave it carte blanche to rebuild its fleet. Worse, Britain had signed it without consulting its League allies, France and Italy, which were also naval powers, so breaking the solidarity the three countries had earlier shown towards Germany.

In October 1935, avid for easy conquests, Mussolini attacked Abyssinia (Ethiopia), expecting a walkover. The Abyssinians fought back – with spears and muskets against aircraft, tanks and poison gas – and appealed to the League of Nations for help. Britain demanded economic sanctions against Italy, but failed to enforce them effectively – in particular, it did not cut vital oil imports to Italy. The result was to turn Mussolini into a potential ally of Nazi Germany, which he had until then considered barbarous with questionable ambitions in the Balkans, without really checking him. Hitler kept studiously neutral in this quarrel, which benefited him so much. Then in February 1936 France ratified a defensive treaty with Soviet Russia, despite bitter domestic opposition to alliance with the dreaded Communists. In response, Hitler marched into the Rhineland on 7 March.

This had long been his aim, for his expansionist ambitions to the east were impossible as long as the French army could advance unchecked into the Ruhr, Germany's industrial heartland. A further stimulus was a sudden shortage of oils and fats in Germany – all available foreign currency going to the rearmament programme – and such a coup would divert Germans' attention from their stomachs. (Göring might claim that Germans would always choose 'guns before butter'

(Frischauer, W. *Goering*, 1951) but most Germans wanted both.) It was a high risk strategy, however, as France had on paper 90 divisions, while Germany could deploy only two. The German high command, especially General Blomberg, was aghast, but Hitler insisted. He later confessed, 'The 48 hours after the march into the Rhineland were the most nerve-racking in my life.' (Schmidt, Paul *Statist auf diplomatischer Bühne*, 1949).

But, as he predicted, the French army did nothing. German troops crossed the Rhine to be welcomed with flowers and flags. The British considered it just the Germans marching 'into their own backyard', and ignored it – apart from Winston Churchill's prophetic but unheeded warnings from the backbenches. In Berlin, Hitler called in the main foreign ambassadors, berated the French for allying with the 'Asiatic power of Bolshevism', meaning Russia, and offered a demilitarization of both sides of the frontier and more disarmament treaties amid his now customary protestations of peace. The Germans swiftly began building a West Wall of fortifications, nicknamed the Siegfried Line, to match the French Maginot Line. It would now soon be impossible for the Western allies to intervene in Germany even if they wanted.

Addressing the cheering Reichstag that same day, Hitler said, 'How hard was the road that I have travelled since January 1933 to free Germany from the dishonourable position in which it found itself and to secure equal rights, without … alienating Germany from the political commonwealth of European nations and without creating new ill feeling from the aftermath of old enmities … Why can we not end this useless strife [between France and Germany] which has lasted centuries? Why not replace it with the rule of reason?' Hitler then dissolved the Reichstag and in the election on 29 March 1936, in a turnout of 99 per cent, 98.85 per cent voted for the Nazi-approved candidates. Even if such Nazi figures are suspiciously high and suggest rigging of the polls, the figures reveal the depth of Hitler's support among the German people at the time. He was far more popular than in 1933.

The outbreak of the Spanish Civil War in July 1936 gave Hitler another golden opportunity. The Germans sent troops, aircraft and tanks to support Franco's attempt to overthrow the Republican government. If these were modest by comparison with Mussolini's armies, the Luftwaffe (airforce) in particular found Spain a marvellous testing ground for its new forces, terror bombing the defenceless Basque town of Guernica on market day. Meanwhile the British and French governments, appalled by the anarchists and Communists on the Republican side, did nothing to help the doomed Republic. By November 1936 German–Italian relations, in contrast, had reached a point where Mussolini could talk of a Rome–Berlin 'axis' around which the rest of Europe could revolve. From then on Germany and Italy called themselves the 'Axis Powers'. One of the two preconditions for Hitler's policy of conquest in the east had been fulfilled.

The Führer and his people – Life inside the Nazi Reich

7

Hitler's Germany was a totalitarian state. The Nazi Party not only crushed all political opposition but also attempted to control every aspect of its subjects' lives. In this Nazi Germany resembled other twentieth-century dictatorships, such as Stalin's Russia and Mao's China, with one exception: there was no nationalization or expropriation of private property. Great industrial combines such as Krupps, the steel maker, remained privately owned. However, as the demands of war became more pressing, this 'freedom' became more apparent than real. The Gestapo (special police) along with the SS provided the typical totalitarian background of terror, but normally most Germans at least passively accepted Nazism. And many were enthusiastic Nazis. What distinguished Nazism was its obsessional racism which led to the Final Solution, the murder of six million Jews.

A central Nazi belief was *Volksgemeinschaft* or people's community, meaning the half-mystical community of all true Germans – 'German' being determined by race, not citizenship or residence. Only those deemed to belong to the 'Aryan' *Herrenvolk* (master race) were Germans – not Jews or Slavs, who were considered *Untermenschen* (subhuman). Nazi racial theories made almost no sense even at the time, when genetics was primitive. Contesting definitions of what constituted a Jew and what an Aryan were supposedly settled by the Nuremberg 'Blood Laws' of November 1935, which stripped Jews of their last rights, outlawing sexual and most other contacts between Germans and Jewish Germans. Anyone with more than one Jewish grandparent was defined as Jewish, even if baptized Christian. Attempts to classify races by phrenology (measuring skulls) or nose shapes proved unsuccessful, despite the SS chief Himmler's fascination with the subject.

For those who passed the 'Aryan' test, Nazism dominated private as well as public life. Every boy from the age of 10 to 18 had to join the *Hitlerjugend* (Hitler Youth) organization. Developed from earlier Nazi youth organizations, this gained full status in December 1936. Almost all German boys' free time was taken up by Hitlerjugend activities, which included endless Nazi indoctrination, marches, rallies, camps, sporting and choral events and pre-military training. The aim was to produce fit young people blindly devoted to their Führer – and in this the system was very succesful. By September 1939 nearly two million German boys had been enrolled in the Hitlerjugend, ready to conquer or to die at Hitler's command. The Nazis liked to boast that the Hitlerjugend broke down class barriers, for the sons of aristocrats, in theory, marched alongside those of the working class. But its spirit was strongly hierarchical, not egalitarian, modelled, like most Nazi institutions, on the army. The *Bund Deutscher Mädel* (League of German Girls), the female counterpart, taught women to be obedient wives and mothers. (Nazis disapproved of women leaving home to work, although during the later part of the war many women had to work in factories or farms.) At the age of 17, an elite of suitably blonde, blue-eyed girls, chosen on Hitler's birthday, joined the *Glaube und Schönheit* (beauty and fidelity) organization.

The DAF (German Workers' Front), inaugurated in May 1933, was the Nazi replacement for trade unions. This subsumed workers into the 'corporate state', in which they had no effective powers. Real wages, after an initial spurt, stagnated, while profits for industrialists soared, but most workers appeared not to mind. What they lost in economic freedom, they gained in security after the horrors of the Depression. 'Hitler has taken away our freedom – our freedom to starve!' went a popular joke. Cheap holidays – sometimes on cruise ships – and rallies added excitement under the slogan of 'Strength through Joy'. By the late 1930s most Germans were, superficially at least, content with the new regime, as revealed not only by obviously susceptible referendum results but by the increase in the birthrate and marriages and the fall in the suicide rate.

Kultur (culture) was vitally important to Germany, which boasted great universities, opera houses and orchestras. The Nazis, being mostly thugs – Goebbels was one of the few exceptions – shared their semi-educated Führer's distrust of educated people. Typical was Göring's brutal quip: 'When I hear the world culture, I reach for my revolver.' But the Nazis could not ignore the arts, and Hitler's own interest in opera, painting, and architecture was genuine if rigidly limited – his aesthetic tastes, it was said, had stopped at about 1890. Nazism tried to control culture, promoting what it liked and destroying the rest. On 10 May 1933 the first 'book burning' took place, when, in scenes that looked spontaneous but were actually highly organized, students, academics and others took books from libraries, bookshops and schools and burnt them in squares throughout Germany, incinerating about 20,000 volumes. High on the list of banned books were those by Jewish writers – including Heine, one of Germany's supreme poets – as well as contemporary enemies of the regime such as Thomas Mann, the Nobel-laureate novelist.

If such deliberate barbarism sent shivers down the spines of some intellectuals, more rushed to sign up as Nazis, such as the poet Gottfried Benn and the writer Gerhart Hauptmann, both eminent in Weimar days. Martin Heidegger, the Existentialist philosopher, joined the Nazis, becoming Nazi rector of Freiburg University and cutting his connections with Edmund Husserl, his part-Jewish teacher. But some German intellectuals – not just Jews – decided to emigrate, including its greatest scientists, notably Albert Einstein. Their emigration enriched the countries they settled in – principally Britain and the USA. Crucially, Germany soon lagged in nuclear physics, vital for the making of nuclear bombs.

The most striking aspect of the new regime were the frequent rallies and marches. Some were filmed by Leni Riefenstahl, a favourite of both Goebbels and Hitler. Glamorous and undeniably talented, Riefenstahl marked an exception to the general Nazi dislike of career women. She became famous through *Triumph of the Will*, her film of the 1934

Nuremberg Rally. In it she brilliantly caught the drama of the event, with its floodlights creating 'cathedrals of light' in the sky. 'I had spent six years in St Petersburg before the [first] War but for grandiose beauty I have never seen a ballet to compare with it,' wrote Sir Nevile Henderson, British ambassador to Berlin (*Future of a Mission*, 1940). She followed with a film of the Berlin Olympics of 1936. Both films opened with shots of heroic ancient Greek statues, before turning to prime Nazi athletes, suggesting that Nazi 'supermen' were the heirs of classical Greece. The 1936 Olympics was made into a showpiece for the regime. Anti-Jewish notices were taken down and foreigners, escorted round Berlin by politely enthusiastic young Nazis, often returned impressed by the New Germany.

Like the Nuremberg rallies, the Olympics' architectural framework was created by young Albert Speer, who became Hitler's court architect and close associate. Speer developed a monumental stripped-down version of neoclassicism, again recalling ancient Greece, executed on a huge scale that suited Hitler's megalomania. Speer's (completed) masterpieces were the Nuremberg Stadium and the Berlin Chancery of 1938–39, both immense buildings with vast rooms, pillars, endless corridors – calculated primarily to over-awe, and of still debated aesthetic value. But most Nazi-favoured art consisted of kitschy recyclings of nineteenth-century academicism, given a brutal edge. Nazi views of contemporary painting were shown by the infamous *Entartete Kunst* (degenerate art) exhibition of 1937. Weimar Germany had been home to some of the most innovative twentieth-century artists, such as Kandinsky, Klee, Otto Grosz and Beckmann. Hitler, however, declared all this degenerate and in the Exhibition of Degenerate Art in Munich, works by such German artists, along with those of Picasso and Mondrian, were juxtaposed with works by lunatics, inviting the Germans to mock them. The exhibition was a huge success, attracting two million visitors. More than 14,500 'degenerate' art works were removed from museums and galleries round Germany, some being sold, some nabbed by senior Nazis, some destroyed.

Music, considered a supreme example of German cultural pre-eminence, was also Nazified. Mendelssohn was banned for being Jewish, while composers like Arnold Schoenberg or Kurt Weil were doubly damned as avant-garde and Jewish (both fled Germany for the USA). But many eminent musicians such as Richard Strauss, the composer, and Herbert Karajan, the conductor, were seduced or bullied into supporting the Nazis, at least initially. (Strauss, with a Jewish daughter-in-law, Jewish librettists such as Stefan Zweig and many Jewish members of his orchestra, soon fell out with the Nazis.)

In April 1939 Germany celebrated Hitler's 50th birthday. If he had died then he would have been remembered as one of the greatest Germans ever. Certainly no earlier ruler had dominated German life so completely. His portrait hung on every wall, his features – calm, determined, resolute, guiding Germany's destiny – stared down from a million posters as a soldier, statesman, animal lover, even as knight in shining armour. The 'German Greeting' – shouting Heil Hitler with upraised arm – became the norm not just among the party faithful but across society, although the army long resisted it. For many Germans, Hitler acquired the aura of a superstar, if not a god. 'If only the Führer knew of it' people would sigh when something went wrong, and he retained this appeal until well into the war. Appearing spotlit at rallies or marches like a secular messiah, he attracted hysterical adulation, especially from women, who reached out to touch him. He enjoyed this form of mass intimacy for he was very much the people's Führer.

Hitler prided himself on his *magnetsiche Kraft* (magnetic power) or personal charisma. His lengthy, firm handshake, combined with a deep, penetrating look from his (rather bulbous) blue eyes, thrilled almost all who met him, turning even sceptics into admirers. It could overcome the objections of powerful characters such as Göring or Mussolini. 'This is the miracle of the age, that you [the German people] have found me among so many millions. And that I have found you, that is Germany's good fortune!' he proclaimed (Baynes, N. *Speeches of Adolf Hitler*, 1942). He seemed to renew not just his popularity but his self-confidence by his speeches, experiencing an almost erotic union with the hundreds of thousands he roused to ecstatic fervour with their endlessly repeated cries of '*Sieg Heil!*' (Hail victory!) In a big speech, he claimed to lose 5–6 lb. (2 kg) in sweat. But the man at the centre of this hysterical personality cult remains strangely void.

'If Hitler had had friends, I would have been his friend,' remarked Speer revealingly (Speer, Albert *Memoirs*, 1977). But Hitler never had real friends. He had had almost no family life since leaving home and in his youth made no friends, preferring instead the company of people he could impress with long monologues in cafés or beerhalls. As he rose to power, he distanced himself even from these beerhall cronies. He liked to claim that he could never marry because he was 'wedded to the German people'. But there were two significant women in Hitler's life, his niece Geli Raubal, daughter of his half-sister Angela, and Eva Braun, daughter of a craftsman.

Twenty years younger than her uncle, Geli first met 'Uncle Alf', as she called him, in 1926 and in 1929 moved into Hitler's spacious new Munich apartment. Flirtatiously attractive, Geli was supposedly studying singing, but Hitler took her around Munich with him all the time. He soon became insanely possessive, threatening to shoot his chauffeur when Geli flirted with him. Geli clearly found this stifling and wanted, in vain, to return to Vienna. When Hitler was away from Munich on 19 September 1931, she was found dead in his apartment, apparently shot with his revolver. There was a huge scandal, enemies saying Hitler had had her killed to prevent her revealing something awful. But he could hardly have chosen a worse way to do so and probably Geli did commit suicide. Hitler suffered a breakdown, disappearing from view for some days, before recovering with typical suddenness.

No woman ever again moved him as Geli had. Her successor, Eva Braun, was a brainless blonde in whom, as Speer warned, 'history will be very disappointed' (*Memoirs*, 1977). Unlike Geli, Eva was obsessed with Hitler – not vice versa – and seemingly content to wait for him in

Munich or the Berghof. Her mindless passivity suited Hitler. 'The greater the man, the more insignificant should be the woman,' he once said (Haste, Cate *Nazis and Women: the Seduction of a Nation*, 2001). His marriage to her just before he took his life in 1945 surprised even close associates, for he hardly saw her in later days. Rumours about Hitler's supposed perversions (sadomasochism and coprophilia) were propagated by enemies such as Otto Strasser but remain rumours. Stories that he had only one genital have been disproved. For Hitler sexual relations, like friendship, probably mattered little compared to the pursuit of power.

Unlike most Nazis, Hitler never drank and was a non-smoker. He even avoided tea and coffee. He was also a vegetarian, which was very unusual at the time. He apparently gave up meat and alcohol after his months in prison. Instead, he drank herbal teas and ate special vegetarian meals tested for poison. He loved cream cakes, however, and at the Berghof, the large house he had built high in the Alps, he would entertain chosen visitors to tea, often charming women, especially, by his schmaltzy courtesy. Then he would stroll around the woodland paths with his beloved Alsatian, Blondi, whom he probably loved more than any human being. This was the only exercise he took, and he often worried about his health. He came to rely on Dr Morrell, a quack doctor who had cured him of eczema, and gave him frequent injections to deal with probably psychosomatic symptoms. These often contained strychnine and belladonna, both highly toxic, aggravating his later physical and psychological decline.

Hitler has been called the 'dilettante dictator', for he could be very idle. Although he had a remarkable memory, being able to grasp and memorize technical details with impressive ease, he had no patience for the minutiae of government, hating to read detailed documents. At times he worked frenziedly far into the night – he was always a night bird, later becoming an insomniac – but more often got through business as fast possible in the late morning before retiring to watch films in his private cinema, including some banned by his government. His special delight was daydreaming about architecture. Even as

Russian armies were approaching Berlin in 1945, he spent hours looking at Speer's megalomaniac models for rebuilding Linz and Berlin. His grand passion, however, remained Wagner. He attended the Bayreuth Wagner Festival every year, listening entranced – senior Nazis accompanying were often seen to yawn. But his favourite music was the Viennese operetta *The Merry Widow* by Franz Lehar.

He seems to have half-believed in astrology, although he also scorned it, and had vague ideas about 'Fate'. 'I go the way that Providence dictates with the assurance of a sleep-walker,' he said in 1936. He had no real religious faith, believing ultimately in a universal but squalid struggle for survival. (For all his talk of the Nordic master race, he was indifferent to the wartime sufferings of actual Germans.) His governing belief was in himself as one of history's extraordinary individuals, a concept probably derived from Friedrich Hegel, the nineteenth-century philosopher who also influenced Marx. 'World History occupies a higher ground than morality ... Irrelevant moral claims must not be allowed to clash with world-historical deeds ... Private virtues – modesty, humility, philanthropy, forbearance – must not be raised against them,' Hegel wrote. Whether or not Hitler read Hegel, such beliefs helped mould his outlook, as did the fiery rhetoric of Nietzsche, who coined the phrase the 'Superman'. (Nazis had to read Nietzsche selectively, however, as Nietzsche admired many Jewish writers.)

Hitler's library contained numerous books on history and military tactics but no novels, no poetry, almost no philosophy – nothing that might have widened his mind or weakened his prejudices. In many ways he was formidably ignorant of the world, which accounts for his misjudgements of Britain and the USA. His ignorance emerged in his endless monologues, often late at night, which taxed the ability of listeners to stay awake. 'Hitler talks, talks, talks, talks,' recorded Ciano, the Italian Foreign Minister about a meeting in April 1942. 'Hitler talked uninterruptedly for an hour and 40 minutes ... on war, peace, religion, philosophy, art and history ... General Jodl, after an epic struggle, finally went to sleep on the divan.' (Ciano, *Diary*, 1947)

In his last years Hitler exhibited many symptoms of paranoia, schizophrenia and psychosis, but such labels inadequately explain the man. He may also have been suffering from Parkinson's Disease from 1943 on, as his hands began trembling uncontrollably. This could have been psychosomatic in origin, as he withdrew deeper into his bunker. Hatred finally dominated his character – of Jews, academics, priests, democrats (he called Churchill a 'bullshit' but admired Stalin's murderous ruthlessness), foreigners, generals who were defeated, modern musicians. In his last years he abandoned the statesmanlike language which had earlier graced his leadership and lapsed back into the gutter language of the beerhall leader, seething with resentment. It was a resentment that he had the power to vent across an entire continent.

8 Preparing for war

The triumphant Berlin Olympics in July 1936 sealed the restoration of German national pride: the Rhineland had been reoccupied, the armed forces were being rebuilt, unemployment had plummeted. Abroad, the Western democracies half-accepted Hitler's protestations of peace and certainly were not concerting effective opposition to him. But for Hitler, all this was just the beginning. As he had rather rashly revealed in *Mein Kampf*, he aimed not just at a revived Germany but at a German empire in the east which would dominate Europe, perhaps the world. This, he accepted, would mean war at some point, a prospect he personally relished. Wartime had been the happiest period of his life and Nazi ideology extolled the virtues of fighting. But, with memories of the First World War's horrors strong both at home and abroad, and Germany relatively weak, he had for long to disguise his expansionist aims from Germans as well as foreigners.

In August 1936 the conscription period in the armed forces was increased to two years, almost doubling the size of the Wehrmacht. At the Nuremberg Rally the following month, Hitler proclaimed a Four Year Plan, and on 18 October gave Göring control of the economy. To make Germany self-sufficient in strategic raw materials, synthetic rubber (buruma) and oil plants were built. That their products proved uncompetitive with imported oil and rubber was unimportant. Germany both lacked the foreign currency for imports – the industries that might have been producing exports were busy making armaments – and needed security of supply in wartime. In a secret memorandum of August 1935 Hitler had talked of being ready for war by 1940. In December 1936 Göring told industrialists that 'no limit on rearmament can be visualized. The only alternatives are war or destruction ... We live in a time when battle is in sight. We are already on the threshold of mobilization ... All that is lacking is the actual shooting.' (*Nuremberg Documents*, 1945–6).

Schacht was still officially Minister for Economy, this wasteful duplication being typical of the Nazi state which rapidly developed overlapping and competing bureaucracies. He grew alarmed at the reckless speed of rearmament – which risked renewed inflation – and in August 1937 resigned against Hitler's wishes. (He remained as titular head of the Reichsbank.) Real economic power now belonged to Göring. He, however, proved incapable of managing the economy – he was already the indolent head of the Luftwaffe – being far more concerned with gaining business for his own Reichswerke H. Göring. (Hitler positively encouraged such corruption at all levels down to the smallest Gauleiter as a way of cementing loyalty to him.) After an executive reorganization in 1938, big corporations like I G Farben took on the running of the chemical industries much more efficiently. Soon they would be running such plants with slave labour inside Auschwitz, the extermination camp.

Hitler wanted to make certain that Italy, diplomatically isolated after her Abyssinian aggression, would accept his future plans for annexing Austria. These were left deliberately vague as to their implementation, for Hitler was a skilled opportunist. A series of diplomatic exchanges culminated with Mussolini, in a special new uniform, visiting Germany in September 1937. He was given an elaborate reception, including a rally in Berlin where the two dictators addressed a crowd of 800,000. A sudden thunderstorm curtailed the rally, soaking Mussolini, but the Duce, visibly impressed by Germany's might, threw in his lot with Hitler. Hitler, for his part, genuinely admired Mussolini, finding him another 'man of the people' like himself – Mussolini's father had been a blacksmith. In November Mussolini added Italy's signature to the Anticomintern Pact (anti-Communist) between Japan and Germany. The coming wartime line-up of Axis powers was complete.

Hitler also secured his own position vis-à-vis the German army, whose upper-class conservativism he distrusted and despised – a feeling requited by the stiff Prussians. On 5 November 1937 Hitler revealed his plans to a secret meeting which included Göring, Field-Marshal

Blomberg the War Minister, Neurath the Foreign Minister and General von Fritsch, Commander in Chief of the army. Hitler declared that Germany's whole future depended on obtaining *Lebensraum* (living space) in central and eastern Europe, starting with Austria and Czechoslovakia; neither overseas colonization nor trade offered acceptable alternatives. Surveying the world scene, he predicted with uncanny accuracy that Britain and France had probably already 'written off' these two states but that war before 1943 was anyway in Germany's interests, when her rearmament would peak. His non-Nazi listeners were perhaps appalled at his naked ambitions, but they were soon ousted.

In January 1938 War Minister Blomberg remarried, Hitler and Göring attending his wedding. But when the police examined his new wife's records, they discovered she had been a prostitute. The Prussian officer corps, shocked by such a misalliance, supported Hitler when he demanded Blomberg's resignation. Göring, who wanted to be Wehrmacht Commander in Chief himself, now produced another dossier purportedly showing that General Fritsch had been involved with a notorious blackmailing homosexual and he too was forced to resign. (Later it became clear that it was another Fritsch who had been blackmailed.) Hitler, seemingly furious with the generals, announced that he himself would become the new Commander in Chief of the Armed Forces, with General Keitel, a remarkably compliant officer, becoming his Chief of Staff. The War Ministry's work was now done by the *Oberkommando der Wehrmacht* (OKW). Sixteen other senior generals were retired and Göring became a field marshal. Hitler used the opportunity to purge the Foreign Service, where Neurath was replaced by Ribbentrop, ousting the last conservatives. Now Nazis dominated the Foreign Service and armed forces.

Soon such scandals were forgotten in foreign policy triumphs. Kurt von Schussnigg, the Austrian Chancellor, inadvertently gave Hitler his pretext for intervening in Austria, despite a treaty of 1936 recognizing Austria's independence. Schussnigg's shaky right-wing coalition had been imprisoning Nazis, along with Socialists, but the Austrian Nazis continued to cause mischief. Plans for a coup were discovered in January, and Schussnig needed Hitler's help to quell the Nazis. On 12 February 1938 he travelled to the Berghof to see the Führer. Hitler bullied him into agreeing to accept Nazis in his cabinet, release imprisoned Nazis and align Austria's economy with Germany's, in an 'evolutionary' approach to unification. Schussnigg, once back in Vienna, changed his mind. Instead, he proclaimed a plebiscite (referendum) on the question 'Do you want a free, Christian, German Austria?' for 13 March.

Hitler, furious at the news, decided to annex Austria. He sent an envoy to Italy to obtain Mussolini's support – needlessly, as Mussolini already had told Ribbentrop that he 'was tired of imposing independence on Austria'. And on 12 March, in reply to a 'request' for help from Austrian Nazis, German troops crossed the frontier, Hitler following them to Linz, where he laid a wreath on his parents' grave. The invaders had an enthusiastic reception and on 14 March Hitler made a triumphant entry into the old imperial capital he had left in ignominy 25 years earlier. Speaking to the crowds from the Hofburg Palace, he said: 'I believe it was God's will to send a youth from here [Austria] into the Reich … to raise him to be a leader of the nation so as to enable him to lead back his homeland into the Reich.' (Baynes, N. *Speeches of Adolf Hitler*, 1942) That same night the SS began the arrests – soon totalling 76,000 – while elderly Jews were forced to scrub pavements with bare, bleeding hands. In a plebiscite held in April throughout the new 'Greater Germany', 99 per cent voted their approval.

Britain and France made merely formal protests, regarding the *Anschluss* (annexation) almost as an internal German affair, but the political situation had been transformed. Vienna, gateway to the Danube basin and Balkans, was in German hands. More pertinently, German troops now almost surrounded Czechoslovakia, the democratic, prosperous but ethnically mixed republic – once part of Austro-Hungary but never of Germany – which was Hitler's next intended victim. The three million plus Germans living in Czechoslovakia – called 'Sudeten Germans', although many did not live in the Sudeten borderlands – provided Hitler with the perfect excuse for his expansionist claims. Although not remotely as ill-treated as they claimed, these Germans had never been happy living in a Czech-dominated state and many supported the local Nazis, now agitating violently for union with Greater Germany. But Czechoslovakia, unlike Austria, had a well-equipped army and alliances with both France and Russia. An attack on it might spark a European war.

This the British and French governments were determined to avoid. Neville Chamberlain, the British Prime Minister, convinced that he alone understood and could settle the dispute, urged the Czechs to make every concession to the Sudeten Germans to avoid France having to honour its alliance, so dragging Britain, its ally, into war. Hitler, however, made increasingly warlike noises throughout the summer, part-bluff, part-genuine. He wanted to dismember Czechoslovakia and relished the prospect of imminent war, although his generals, aware of the unreadiness of the Wehrmacht, were secretly appalled. In July Chamberlain sent a special envoy to Prague to press President Benes to be even more flexible, but to no avail. On 12 September at the Nuremberg Rally Hitler made a violent speech about the Czechs, provoking an abortive rising by the Sudeten Nazis. Chamberlain then offered to fly to Germany – the first time he had ever flown – to discuss matters with Hitler personally. On 15 September Hitler met Chamberlain at the Berghof to decide the fate of Europe.

Ranting, Hitler declared he would not 'tolerate any longer a small, second-rate country treating the mighty thousand-year Reich as inferior', which he would obliterate (Schmidt, Paul *Statist auf diplomatischer Bühne*, 1949). Then he suddenly became reasonable and agreed to annex only the Sudetenland. Chamberlain flew home and persuaded the British, French and unhappy Czech governments to accept this proposal, and to dissolve Czech alliances with France and Russia. But when he again flew to Germany on 22 September, Hitler had apparently changed his mind. Brandishing (faked) reports of Czech 'atrocities' against Germans, Hitler threatened war if the German army could not occupy the Sudetenland by 1 October. Shaken, Chamberlain returned home, and the British cabinet decided, with huge reluctance, to support France in the case of war. The navy was mobilized and bomb shelters dug in Hyde Park. (Britain expected massive bombing raids immediately, but in fact the Luftwaffe was still far too weak to attack Britain.) On 26 September Hitler made a fanatically bellicose speech, but the next day, watching Germans silently turning their backs on an armoured division rolling through Berlin, he realized his own people were not yet ready for war.

Mussolini, observing events anxiously, now proposed a meeting in Munich of Germany, Italy, France and Britain – excluding the Czechs and Russians. Hitler, brilliantly assessing his democratic opponents' weaknesses, realized that Chamberlain and Daladier, the French Premier, lacked any will to fight, and proved adamant. Late on the night of 29 September it was agreed that Germany should take all the Sudetenland plus other areas, crippling Czechoslovakia. On 1 October German troops occupied the Sudetenland, being impressed by the Czech fortifications. Soon after, Hungary, then Poland, helped themselves to parts of the defenceless state with German encouragement. Hitler might publicly declare he had 'no more territorial demands in Europe' but privately he called the Munich agreement 'an undreamt of triumph' and his opponents 'worms'. Chamberlain returned home boasting of 'peace in our time' and was greeted by jubilant crowds, Churchill's being one of the few dissenting voices.

'Peace' did not last long. In March 1939 Hitler summoned the Czech President Hacha (Benes had resigned) to Berlin where he was bullied into signing away his country's independence. The Germans badly wanted the Škoda arms industry and Czech gold reserves, and Hitler hated even the remnant of Czechoslovakia. On 15 March German troops entered Prague, watched by silent Czechs, and Hitler spent the night in Hradschin Castle. This time there was no excuse about

German minorities; this was naked aggression. Britain hurriedly guaranteed the borders of Poland, next in the firing line. The immediate issue was Danzig (now Gdansk). This important port had been made a 'Free City' after 1918. Predominantly German, it was divided from the rest of Germany by the 'Polish Corridor', a strip of land connecting Poland to the sea at Gdynia (see map, p. 15). Hitler tried once to persuade Poland to accept a road and rail link and the return of Danzig to Germany (as before 1918), offering territorial compensation elsewhere. but the Poles refused, proudly if rashly. Enraged by both Poland and Britain, Hitler gave his generals orders to prepare to invade Poland on 1 September and tore up the Anglo–German naval treaty. But there was another, highly significant player which had to be taken into account.

Poland's giant eastern neighbour, the Soviet Union, was distrusted by the Poles and regarded as a pariah by the west. As the home of Bolshevism, it was also hated by Hitler, who anyway sought German Lebensraum there, but Hitler could be surprisingly pragmatic. The Poles would not let Russian troops enter their country even as allies and the British and French were reluctant to ally themselves with the Communists. In June a Franco–British mission was sent to Moscow – but by slow boat, not plane. Stalin, the Soviet leader, aware of how the British had let down the Czechs, distrusted the Western Allies' motives, suspecting they were trying to embroil him in a war with Germany. (Russia was already involved in a minor, undeclared Far Eastern war with the Japanese along the banks of the Amur River.) Hitler, who had withdrawn to Obersalzberg after briefing his generals in May, scented an opportunity to avoid a two-front war, a recurrent German nightmare. Ribbentrop accordingly began to sound the Russians out, finding them tough going at first.

On 14 August Ribbentrop asked Stalin directly to receive him in Moscow, saying, 'There is no question between the Baltic and Black Seas which cannot be settled to the complete satisfaction of both countries.' (*Documents on German Foreign Policy*, 1948). On 23 August

Ribbentrop flew to Moscow, bastion of the Nazi arch-enemy. He got on very well with the Soviets, and by that evening they had drawn up a Nazi–Soviet Non-Aggression Pact. Added to the public treaty were secret protocols dividing up eastern Europe between Germany and the Soviet Union. The Baltic States (Latvia, Estonia, Lithuania), Finland and eastern Poland fell into the Soviet sphere. Russia would supply Germany with vital raw materials in exchange for manufactured goods. Ribbentrop returned swiftly home to be hailed as a new Bismarck.

The news of this bizarre new friendship astounded the world. (At the British Foreign Office it earned the joke 'all their isms are wasms'.) Suddenly Germany was in a far stronger position. Hitler continued to negotiate, indicating he might accept a second Munich. But this time the British would not force the Poles to surrender. On 1 September at dawn, the German attack on Poland began, overwhelming the ill-equipped and outnumbered if brave Poles. On 3 September, after their ultimatums to Germany to withdraw had lapsed, Britain and France declared war. Hitler, receiving the news in the Chancery, according to an interpreter present, 'sat absolutely silent and unmoving. After a while, he turned to Ribbentrop, who had remained by the window. "What now?" asked Hitler with an angry glare, as if implying that Ribbentrop had misled him about the probable British reaction' (Schmidt, Paul *Statest auf Diplomatischer Bühne*, 1949). The war he had so often threatened had begun. It would end only with his death, along with tens of millions of others.

9 Early victories

Six and a half years of accelerating rearmament had given Germany the most modern if not the largest army in Europe (the Russian and even French armies outnumbered it on paper). It could deploy 51 divisions, including five new *Panzer* (armoured) divisions plus four motorized divisions, with equally large reserve forces, while the Luftwaffe had 4,000 modern aircraft and 260,000 men. Only the navy was unready, but even it now included three heavily armed 'pocket battleships' – so called because theoretically they observed the 10,000-ton limit of the Versailles Treaty – and 47 U-boats (submarines). In 1939, unlike in 1914, Germany would not be fighting on two fronts, thanks to the Non-Aggression Pact. Also, with Russian-supplied raw materials, Germany should be less affected by a British blockade. As Hitler had been warned, Germany was unprepared for a long war, lacking adequate reserves of most munitions, but he intended to avoid a war of attrition like the First World War. He appeared before the Reichstag in military uniform, saying he would not put it off until final victory or death – one promise he kept. From then on the private man Adolf Hitler, never prominent, disappeared ever further behind the public persona of the warlord and Führer.

The Polish campaign proved brief. Attacking from north, south (from Slovakia) and west, German troops launched their first *Blitzkrieg* (lightning war). Armoured columns burst through the Polish lines and surrounded its armies in classic 'pincer tactics', while overhead dive-bombers, the JU-87 'Stuka', spread terror and chaos far behind the lines. The Polish army was outnumbered, outmanoeuvred and outgunned despite desperate courage – at one stage its cavalry charged Panzers. Its small airforce was crippled within two days, allowing the Luftwaffe to bomb Warsaw and other cities unchecked. By 15 September the Polish army had disintegrated, on 19 September Hitler entered Danzig in triumph and on the 25th he watched the Luftwaffe pulverize Warsaw, which then surrendered. The Russians occupied their allotted zone of Poland on 17 September, shooting retreating Polish troops. Meanwhile in the west the French hardly moved against the Siegfried Line, defended by reserve German forces, while the RAF dropped nothing more than leaflets on Germany. (Proposals to bomb Ruhr industries were rejected because they were 'private property'.)

After his cheap victory – cheap for the Germans – Hitler ordered the total destruction of Polish civic society, killing intellectuals, teachers, priests and other potential leaders. At Stalin's insistence, he dropped ideas of creating a rump Polish vassal state. Instead, northern and western Poland was annexed to the Reich, the millions of Poles living there being uprooted and deported to the 'Government-General' of south-east Poland, where many starved to death. On 6 October Hitler made a speech offering peace to Britain and France but, fired by success, he was already planning an offensive in the west. He wanted to start in November with a preventive attack on (neutral) Holland and Belgium. To his generals he stressed the importance of deploying armoured divisions so that they did not get 'lost in the endless rows of houses in Belgium' but retained their mobility.

But bad weather prevented any offensives that year; meanwhile other events drew Hitler's attention northward. By the Nazi–Soviet pact, Finland was in the Soviet sphere. Stalin wanted to annex the Karelian isthmus to strengthen the defences around Leningrad (St Petersburg), but the Finns refused. On 30 November Russia attacked, expecting a walkover. It proved to be a fiasco. The Finns, better equipped and more mobile, repelled the Russian attacks repeatedly. The Germans, watching uncomfortably, did nothing, but Britain and France began to consider intervening via Norway. Allied intervention in Scandinavia threatened Germany's vital supplies of iron ore from Sweden. To pre-empt this, Hitler decided to seize Norway, whose ports could also provide U-boat bases for naval warfare against Britain, and discussed plans for a coup with Vidkun Quisling, a Norwegian Nazi. When the

British intercepted the German prison-ship *Altmark* in Norwegian waters and rescued British prisoners on 17 February, Hitler was enraged. Although the Finns signed an armistice with Russia in March, which reduced chances of Allied intervention, he decided to attack by sea on 9 April, occupying Denmark at the same time. Everything depended on surprise, for Hitler was risking almost the whole German fleet, far smaller than Britain's.

Denmark surrendered at once, airborne troops seized many Norwegian airfields while the navy landed troops all the way up the coast as far as Narvik. But the cruiser *Blücher* was sunk in Oslo Fjord, Quisling's coup failed dismally, the king and cabinet escaping to Britain, and British troops were soon landed. Despite British superiority by sea, however, German air supremacy ensured German victory, the last British troops withdrawing in June with heavy losses. Hitler had taken an obsessively close interest in every detail of the campaign in a way that would later drive his generals to distraction. His attention, meanwhile, returned to the west.

The first German plan for an attack on France had been a variant on that of 1914, dictated partly by the supposedly impregnable Maginot Line from the Swiss to Belgian frontiers, with an offensive through Belgium. But this plan fell into Allied hands in January through an air crash. General von Manstein now proposed that, instead of the main punch of the German attack being on the right, aiming for the Channel ports, it should be on the left, encircling the French and British armies on either side. Hitler adopted this plan, against the advice of most of his generals, in March. It was to produce his greatest victory.

The Anglo–French forces facing Hitler's in May 1940 were marginally superior in numbers, even having more tanks – 3,200 against 3,000 German. But the Germans used armour in a wholly new way, grouped now into ten fast Panzer divisions. Coupled with parachutists and glider troops, whose use Hitler had personally planned, and closely supported by aircraft acting as artillery, this revolutionized warfare. At dawn on 10 May the Germans attacked France, Luxembourg, Belgium and Holland. The great Belgian fortress of Eben Emael was seized by parachute and glider troops within hours. In Holland, parachutists seized Rotterdam airfield and the main bridges. When the city was summoned to surrender on 14 May, the Luftwaffe bombed it during the parley – possibly by mistake – killing 980 civilians, and it promptly capitulated, as did Holland the next day. Meanwhile, British and French armies pushed north into Belgium to meet the advancing Germans. In doing so, they were trapped.

General Rundstedt's army group, with eight Panzer divisions, the bulk of the German armour, had attacked through the Ardennes on 10 May. Thought impassable because heavily wooded, this section was lightly defended, and the German Panzers raced across it on 12 May. On 14 May the first tanks led by General Rommel were north of Sedan, the next day they crossed the River Meuse and by the 20 May General Guderian's columns had reached the coast at Abbeville, cutting off the French and British armies in Belgium. Millions of refugees streaming south-west clogged the roads, making French reinforcements difficult. But there were almost no reinforcements, as the French Commander in Chief, General Gamelin, admitted on 16 May. Much of the French army was still sitting in the Maginot Line. On 28 May Belgium capitulated and the Allied armies had to retreat towards Dunkirk.

Hitler, meanwhile, was worrying about the speed of his armies' advance and dangers to their flanks from counter-attacks. General Halder noted in his diary for 17 May, 'Führer is terribly nervous. Frightened by his own success, he is afraid to take chances and would rather rein us in.' On 24 May, Hitler ordered Guderian's troops to halt for 48 hours – giving the British time to start evacuating 338,000 troops from the beaches in the 'miracle of Dunkirk'. On 5 June the Germans launched a massive new attack south, overrunning the rest of France swiftly. On 14 June Paris fell. On the 16th Marshal Pétain, the hero of the First World War, formed a new government to negotiate an armistice.

Photographs of Hitler receiving the news of the French surrender on 22 June show him almost dancing with joy. He had achieved in six weeks what the Kaiser's empire had not in over four years: total victory in the west, putting him on a level with Bismarck or Napoleon. Although aided by luck, he had won by relying on his own judgement and intuition, rather than his generals' advice, and now was hailed as the supreme warlord, the greatest German in history. Such acclaim dangerously boosted his already overwhelming self-confidence, while temporarily quelling his generals' doubts.

Hitler, aware that the French fleet was still scattered all round the Mediterranean, rebuffed Mussolini's demand for French territories – Italy had only entered the war on 10 June – but humiliatingly made the French sign the Armistice in the same rail carriage at Compiègne in which the Germans had surrendered 22 years earlier. Northern and western France was occupied by German troops, but the rest was left under a puppet government based in Vichy, headed by Pétain. Visiting Paris for the first time as a tourist–conqueror on 28 June, Hitler went up the Eiffel Tower, admiring Napoleon's tomb in the Invalides and the Opéra. 'Paris remains one of the jewels of Europe,' he admitted (Hitler, Adolf *Table Talk*, 1952). Returning to Berlin, he was greeted ecstatically with flowers and peels of bells.

Hitler had just one problem: the British, who under their new, indomitable Prime Minister Churchill showed no signs of asking for peace. On 3 July British ships sank part of the French fleet in Oran rather than let it fall into German hands. On 19 July, speaking to the Reichstag, Hitler made an apparently genuine peace offer, warning that if not accepted 'a great Empire will be destroyed'. Three days earlier, however, Hitler had ordered 'Operation Sea Lion', the invasion of Britain. The German navy lacked the ships to transport the 40 divisions the army demanded, but Göring promised that the Luftwaffe would crush the RAF, cow the British and make a large land invasion unnecessary. On 13 August, his 'Operation Eagle' began with 1,500 aircraft.

The RAF was the Luftwaffe's equal in fighters if not bombers, with 800 Hurricanes and Spitfires, while British aircraft production exceeded Germany's. The British had two technical advantages: radar, which they had pioneered and which the Germans long failed to appreciate fully, and the Ultra decoding machines, which enabled British codebreakers at Bletchley to decipher the secret German Enigma code and read Luftwaffe orders. Even so the Battle of Britain was touch and go. By early September the Luftwaffe seemed about to overwhelm southern English air defences when it switched from bombing airfields to a mass raid on London on 7 September. This, partly a retaliation to a (tiny) British raid on Berlin, gave the RAF a vital respite. On 15 September it broke up the Luftwaffe's attack on London which by then was burning day and night. The Germans never again attempted daylight raids, though the 'Blitz', the nightly bombing of British cities, continued into 1941. On 17 September Hitler abandoned Operation Sea Lion. He had suffered his first major defeat, but already he was looking east.

Hitler had wanted to attack Russia that autumn – in June Russia had annexed the three Baltic states and part of Romania, enraging him – but his forces were unready and Mediterranean events distracted him. Italian forces invading Greece in October 1940 were repelled, Italian attacks on British-held Egypt from Libya were equal failures, the British advancing into Libya. Hitler had to dispatch the 'Afrika Corps' to Libya under Rommel, who routed the British in April 1941. But the Spanish would not co-operate by attacking Gibraltar, despite Hitler going all the way to Hendaye on the Spanish frontier to meet its dictator Franco. Hungary, Romania and Yugoslavia were coerced into letting German troops enter them en route for Greece when a coup in Belgrade on 27 March overthrew its pro-German government. Hitler, enraged, determined to exterminate Yugoslavia. 'Operation Punishment' began on 6 April with the Luftwaffe bombing a defenceless Belgrade, killing 17,000 civilians. Within ten days Yugoslavia had surrendered, as did Greece a week later. British troops had to withdraw hastily and Crete soon fell to German parachutists, with many British soldiers captured.

But for Hitler this was only a sideshow. German troops returned north to join the armies massing along the Russian frontier as he finalized plans for his great vision: the drive east for *Lebensraum*, code-named Barbarossa (Italian 'red beard', nickname of the great medieval German emperor Frederick I). 'The world will hold its breath,' Hitler declared as three million men, the largest force ever known, with 3,550 tanks and 3,500 aircraft, moved up to attack on 22 June. Despite many warnings – from his own agents besides Churchill – Stalin refused to accept the imminence of invasion. Russian troops were totally unprepared, there was no general mobilization, Russian aircraft were neatly lined up inviting attack.

At first, the German Blitzkrieg again appeared invincible. Most of the huge Soviet airforce was destroyed in the first ten days, as was most Soviet armour. Minsk, 300 miles from the frontier, fell to the Germans on 28 June, Smolensk, two-thirds of the way to Moscow, on 16 July. Russian lines were repeatedly pierced by German armoured columns which then attacked from the rear while German bombers struck far ahead. But, uniquely, the Russians fought on with grim desperation, even if surrounded and out of ammunition, using bayonets and knives. As the Germans advanced, fanning out into the hugeness of Russia, their lines growing thinner and their communications stretched, they could not prevent some Russian formations escaping east. Hitler had divided his armies into three huge groups: a northern one aimed at Leningrad, a central group headed for Moscow, and a southern group at Ukraine. Guderian, commanding half the central group's panzers, wanted to push on after capturing Smolensk to Moscow. But Hitler had other ideas and diverted Panzers north to attack Leningrad and south to take Ukraine.

This decision may have cost Hitler the war in the east. While German armies reached Leningrad early in September, beginning an epic 900-

day siege, and Kiev fell on 18 September with losses of 525,000 Russians – 'the biggest battle in the history of the world!' claimed Hitler – Moscow, centre of the Russian rail network as well as the capital, was saved. When the German central offensive resumed in early October, it faced increasingly tough resistance, although it drove ever closer to Moscow. Then autumn rains began and German tanks became bogged down in a sea of mud, before the temperature in November plummeted. As Hitler had banked on a three-month summer campaign, the Germans had no winter clothing and began freezing. Soon there were hundreds of thousands of cases of frostbite. Even German tanks and aircraft froze as the temperature fell, at times to -65° C. Still the Germans advanced, until they were only 40 miles from the capital. Stalin had assembled 58 fresh divisions, including the crack Siberian divisions, to defend Moscow. On 5 December the Russians launched a devastating counter-offensive, which the Germans had not believed possible. The German offensive turned into a retreat.

Like many – not just in Germany – Hitler had under-estimated Russian resilience. As a result, he faced prolonged war on two fronts. On 7 December 1941 came news of the surprise Japanese attack on the US fleet at Pearl Harbor. Thrilled at the entry of the Japanese – whom he considered invincible – into the war, Hitler also hastened to declare war on the US four days later. Germany, which six months before had faced merely a Britain unable to harm it significantly, was fighting the two greatest potential military powers on earth.

10 Europe under the swastika

The rapid conquests of 1939–41 giving Hitler control of Europe from the Atlantic to central Russia presented problems as well as opportunities. While he had long dreamed about German conquests in the east, he had thought far less about western Europe. After conquering the west, German troops plundered French vineyards while their officers ate in the smartest Parisian restaurants. Unabashed plundering was common in the highest ranks, Göring seizing many great art works for his own collection. 'The real profiteers of this war are ourselves and out it we shall come bursting with fat. We will … take everything we can make use of. And if others protest, I don't give a damn!' Hitler proclaimed with customary crudeness if unusual honesty. But longer term German plans for Western European countries, considered inferior yet 'Aryan', had a few apparently positive aspects, with talk of a new Europe without unemployment. A very different fate awaited German conquests to the east, whose Slav inhabitants were destined to become Germany's slaves or to be exterminated.

The 'Greater German Reich' – incorporating Austria, the Czech lands, much of Poland, Luxembourg, Alsace-Lorraine, parts of Belgium – was to dominate most European states. These had initially to adopt their political and economic systems to the Reich's, but might for a time play a subordinate role in the Europe of the Nazi 'New Order'. As long as Britain remained at war – which few in 1940 expected to be for long – a German occupation force of 40 divisions in the west was necessary. Ultimately Hitler intended to incorporate all suitably 'Nordic' Europeans in a greater Reich north of the Alps – Rotterdam would become Germany's chief port, for example – while Italy had free rein in the Mediterranean.

France was Germany's most important Western conquest, economically and strategically. From its shores the Luftwaffe launched its chief attacks on Britain, and the ports of Brest and St Nazaire became key U-boat bases for the Battle of the Atlantic; from its farms and factories the Germans sucked the supplies needed to continue the war. After the Armistice in June 1940 Marshal Pétain, new head of state, was allowed to withdraw his government to Vichy in central France – chosen for its abundant hotels – from which he theoretically ruled about 45 per cent of France. The remainder, including Paris and the Atlantic and Channel coasts, was occupied by the Wehrmacht. The Fascist Vichy state, its Prime Minister the pro-German Laval, vowed to maintain the 'honour' of France by active collaboration under the slogans '*Travail, Famille, Patrie*' (Work, Family, Fatherland). Allowed to retain an army of 100,000 in France, Vichy also controlled the large French overseas empire in Africa and Asia with its armies and fleets, which gave it some bargaining powers. However, more than two million French soldiers remained prisoners-of-war in Germany, offsetting this. After the Anglo–American landings in North Africa in November 1942, German troops occupied even this 'free' zone, to forestall Allied attacks on southern France.

Real power throughout France, however, as in all occupied countries, always rested with the Germans. They set exorbitant 'occupation costs' of 300 million French francs a day, rising to 500 million after 1942. Often they took this in kind, from capital assets such as industrial machinery to 320 million bottles of wine per year. Above all, the Germans seized food. This led to widespread malnutrition throughout France. Official rations only provided 1,200 calories per day at best and was even lower in other occupied countries. Soon food, clothing and fuel were only available at black market prices far beyond most people's reach. The Germans also took forced labour from France, as from all occupied countries. With the connivance of Laval, who hoped to exchange them for freed prisoners of war, 1.7 million Frenchmen ended up working in often appalling conditions in Germany. In all, seven million foreign workers were conscripted by Germans by 1944, many being effectively slaves.

Across Western Europe, active resistance was at first limited (the powerful Communist parties collaborated passively until the invasion of the Soviet Union, from which they took their orders). Few French people heard the ringing appeals of Charles de Gaulle in June 1940, broadcast from London – 'La France a perdu une bataille! La France n'a pas perdu la guerre!' (France has lost a battle, France has not lost the war). De Gaulle had only become a minister just before France's fall, and until mid-1943 was not recognized by the Allies as leader of the Free French. (President Roosevelt in particular distrusted him.) Once the whole of France was directly occupied by the Germans and they began rounding up more men for forced labour in the Reich – even seizing 1,000 French gendarmes in Marseilles – resistance became widespread and especially open in the Maquis, the bush-covered Massif Central mountains. The German reacted savagely. Over 30,000 French hostages were killed in retaliation even before the great rising before D-day, when some 200,000 lightly armed troops mobilized, attacking railways, roads and bridges. Their actions helped slow down German troops reaching Normandy by vital days. General Eisenhower, the supreme Allied commander said, perhaps exaggerating, that they were worth 15 divisions to the Allies.

All the occupied countries came to resist, but in differing ways. In Denmark, which the Nazis considered 'their little Aryan brother', a surprising degree of freedom was at first permitted. Elections in 1942 even returned a Social Democrat government, the King was still head of state – snubbing the Nazis by ignoring their salutes – and resistance was correspondingly small. But even here the Germans occupied the country fully in 1943, imposing an increasingly hard regime and provoking unarmed resistance. As in flat, densely populated Holland, armed resistance was very difficult. By contrast in Greece, brutally treated from the start, the combined resistance, despite divisions between Communists and monarchists, blew up the vital

Gorgopotamos rail viaduct in November 1942, cutting the Afrika Korps' chief supply route. About 45,000 Greek civilians were killed in reprisals for this. The most notorious reprisal happened in Bohemia, after the assassination of Heydrich, the Reich protector, in May 1942. About 1,500 Czechs were killed immediately, some 3,000 Jews were sent to the extermination camps and then, after a few days, the population of the village of Lidiče were rounded up, all the men shot and the women and children sent to the death camps, and the village razed to the ground.

Hitler from the first insisted on extreme measures, spurning 'political' measures such as trying to win the passive co-operation of conquered nations. The infamous 'Nacht und Nebel' (night and fog) order issued in December 1941 was his idea, designed to terrify whole populations. The death penalty would be automatic – even lifelong hard labour being thought inadequate – for any of the loosely defined 'offences against the Reich'. Persons arrested would simply 'vanish' into night and fog, lack of knowledge of their fate adding to their family's fears. All acts of resistance should be ascribed to Communists and 50 to 100 hostages were to be executed for every German soldier killed. This ratio was often exceeded.

Far more terrible than Western Europe's fate was that of the Slavs in Poland and the conquered Soviet territories Before the launch of Barbarossa, Hitler warned his generals that 'the war against Russia will be such that it cannot be conducted in a chivalrous fashion. This struggle of ideologies and racial differences must be conducted with unprecedented, merciless and unrelenting harshness.' Hitler's stated aim in most of European Russia was to 'Germanize the country by the settlement of Germans and treat the natives as redskins' – that is, to reduce their population by deliberate genocide. The rest would be kept subservient, ill-fed, badly housed and educated 'just enough to understand road signs, so as not to be run over by our vehicles'. Hitler envisaged fortified German settlements as far as the Urals, distinct from Russian cities which would be destroyed. Other suitably Nordic peoples – Dutch, Flemings, Norwegians, even English – would supplement German settlers. These Nordic forts would be connected by Autobahns and fast double-decker trains Outside them, Russians would toil in even worse conditions than under the Tsars or Stalin. But at least 30 million Slavs needed to be killed first. A direct consequence of this attitude was the maltreatment of millions of Soviet prisoners-of-war. Herded together behind barbed war, they were literally left to starve until, at the end of 1941, the Germans realized they needed their labour and decided to work some of them to death in concentration camps.

At first many in the conquered western parts of the Soviet Union, especially in the Baltic states and in the Ukraine, which had suffered terribly from Stalin's murderous 'collectivization' programme, welcomed German rule, thinking anything must be better than Stalinism. Alfred Rosenberg, the mystical Nazi who became 'Minister for the East', had plans for semi-independent Ukrainian and Baltic states which might have won collaboration. But Himmler, head of the SS empire, which by then incorporated most of the German police, had genocidal ideas in tune with Hitler's. Immediately behind the advancing army in 1941 rode the *Einsatzgruppen*, SS special squads, who rounded up and killed anyone deemed a 'commissar' or Communist as well as all Jews. In practice this gave the SS a licence to murder everyone they wanted. A report, with typical ghastly precision, from Einsatzgruppe A for February 1942 records that it had executed '1,064 commissars, 56 partisans, 653 mental cases, 44 Poles, 29 Russian prisoners-of-war, 5 Gypsies, 1 Armenian and 136,421 Jews'. Inevitably, such brutality encouraged rather than prevented growing Russian resistance, in turn triggering more reprisals. By 1943 guerrilla groups had formed across much of occupied Russia, controlling large areas where the terrain favoured them, such as the Belorussian forests, greatly hampering the German army. About 25 million Russians are thought to have died in the war, the majority civilians killed by the Germans.

Even so, nearly one million Russians ended up fighting on the German side. This was often involuntary, the alternative being literally death. These *Osttruppen* (Eastern troops) were distrusted by the Nazis, especially by Hitler. Redeployed in the west, many found themselves at the end of the war handed back to the avenging Soviets by the Allies. Vlasov, a Russian general who helped defend Moscow in 1941, changed sides after capture in 1942, winning some support from German officers aware that the war was not being won easily. But Hitler, distrusting any separatist attempts, squashed Vlasov's plan for a national Russian army and Vlasov ended his life defending Prague against the Germans.

Hitler's principal victims, however, were his lifelong scapegoats, the Jews. The Jewish population of pre-war Germany had been relatively small, less than 500,000 before emigration reduced it further. While the annexation of Austria and the Czech lands in 1938–39 more than doubled this, anti-Jewish measures were spasmodic until the war, such as *Kristalnacht* (broken glass night) in November 1938, when many Jewish premises were attacked 'spontaneously' by SA bands across Germany. With the conquest of Poland in 1939, another three million Jews fell into Nazi hands. The Nazis, often cheered on by the Poles, began by crowding all Polish Jews into ghettos in Warsaw, Krakow and other cities, where many died from typhus and other diseases. They could not die fast enough for the Nazis, however. Differing Nazi plans for Europe's Jews included sending them to Madagascar (a French colony), or beyond the Urals, when Russia had been conquered. The Einsatzgruppen probably killed nearly a million Russian Jews in 1941–42, with machine guns, rifles and even axes, often assisted enthusiastically by local people. The most infamous massacre was at Babi Yar outside Kiev, when 33,000 Jews – ordered to assemble for 'resettlement' – were marched to a ravine on the edge of the city, stripped of their clothing and shot in the head, their bodies being thrown in the ditch and covered with thin layers of lime and earth. Soon gases from their decomposing bodies bubbled up and the corpses had to be exhumed and burnt.

Such messy murders were found by Himmler – who almost fainted witnessing one 'action' – to be inefficient, and other solutions to the 'Jewish Problem' were sought. At the Wannsee Conference in Berlin in January 1942, the Nazi chiefs decided to murder every single European Jew, although those deemed useful to the war effort (such as the great Italian writer Primo Levi, an industrial chemist) were to be worked to death rather than murdered outright. This was the 'Final Solution', Hitler's most monstrous and most revealing monument. The Germans built special extermination camps across Poland at Chelmno, Treblinka, Sobibor, Belsec and most notoriously at Auschwitz.

These differed from earlier concentration camps in that their prime, though not sole, purpose was mass murder – German industry also set up factories there to exploit the slave labour available. Jewish men, women and children from as far away as Thessalonica in Greece were rounded up and transported huge distances in cattle trucks – without water or food, many died on the long rail journey. On arrival, those found by doctors to be too sick to work went straight to the gas chambers, where Zyklon B gas killed them in 5–10 minutes. Their bodies were then examined, gold fillings being extracted from their teeth and collected, sometimes women's long hair being shorn off, and their corpses were burnt in huge crematoria. Auschwitz could 'process' 12,000 people a day, the other camps rather fewer. More than one million human beings are estimated to have been murdered in Auschwitz. In total, about 6 million out of the 8.5 million Jews living in Europe were killed by the Nazis, the numbers of survivors varying markedly according to country. Holland saw almost all its Jews taken but the Danes managed to get theirs away to Sweden by small boats. Vichy France proved remarkably eager to hand over its Jewish citizens but Hungary protected its Jews until the final German occupation. Other groups the Nazis exterminated included 200,000 Gypsies, along with homosexuals, Jehovah's Witnesses and those considered physically or mentally abnormal.

Beyond any shadow of doubt, Hitler himself was not only aware of, but was directly responsible for the Final Solution, although he signed no documents about it. Murderous, obsessive hatred of Jews was the strongest, most consistent aspect of his character, revealed in a thousand speeches, and he repeatedly described Jews as 'lice' who should only be killed. In *Mein Kampf* he had already talked of 'holding twelve or fifteen thousand Hebrew corrupters of the people under poison gas'. He may not have bothered with the details of the Final Solution but he never liked dealing with the details of anything except weapons. Anti-Semitism already had a long and shameful history in Christian Europe, where for centuries Jews were intermittently persecuted. But under the leadership of Hitler – who despised Christianity as a 'Jewish' religion – most of occupied Europe now became in some way involved in the organized mass murder that was the Holocaust.

11 The turn of the tide

Although Ribbentrop pointed out that Germany was not bound by treaty with Japan to attack the US, Hitler had reasons for doing so. Under President Roosevelt the US had moved from being a neutral friendly to Britain to being almost an undeclared belligerent. 'Lend Lease', signed in March 1941, supplied on credit an increasing flow of materials, including arms, to Britain, and by late 1941 also to Russia. By August 1941 ships carrying these across the Atlantic were at times escorted by US Navy vessels as far as Iceland. In September Roosevelt issued a 'Shoot at Sight' order to US ships, leading to armed clashes between U-boats and American ships in the autumn of 1941. But before Pearl Harbor, Roosevelt could not persuade Congress to declare war, while Admiral Raeder, the German navy chief, in vain urged Hitler to let German U-boats retaliate.

Hitler assumed that the US would be too busy in the Pacific to intervene against Germany, allowing him to finish off Russia and then, with 'blockade-proof' Lebensraum, outface the Western Allies. While Hitler over-estimated Japanese power, which had built up but could not sustain a large battle fleet, he grossly underestimated the American potential. He also misunderstood American society, believing his own propaganda that Roosevelt was a corrupt plutocrat with little support and that many Americans, being of German descent, really supported Germany, not Britain, and anyway lacked discipline and courage.

At first, events in the west favoured Germany. Allowed to wage unrestricted war, U-boats began sinking unescorted US ships right down to the Caribbean. In March and again in June U-boats, operating mainly from bomb-proof 'pens' in Brittany, sank 800,000 tons of shipping, more than all Allied shipyards together could replace.

Germany was threatening to win the 'Battle of the Atlantic', the vital struggle to keep Britain supplied and to convey US forces across the ocean to attack Germany. While the first USAAF bombing raids on Germany only started in August 1942 with just 18 planes, the RAF had already launched its first '1,000 bomber raid' on Cologne in May. But such early attacks were too inaccurate to damage Germany seriously. They even helped Nazi propaganda, for they aroused hostility to the Western Allies for the first time in the German people.

Hitler, however, was more concerned in early 1942 with his disintegrating Eastern Front. As Russian counter-attacks developed along the over-extended line, some German generals suggested retreating right back to Poland, which drove Hitler into a fury. Instead, he insisted all units should stand and fight, adopting 'hedgehog' type formations if surrounded, personally telephoning field commanders to give orders and encouragement. This unconventional approach probably saved the German army from disaster. By the time fighting ceased in the spring mud, the front was only pushed back about 100 miles. The Germans had suffered about 1,150,000 casualties, a quarter fatal, but the Russians had suffered vastly more – about 6 million, about half fatal.

Several of Hitler's best generals, including Guderian and Brauchitsch, the Commander in Chief of the army, were sacked for questioning his 'No Retreat' orders. Hitler, never willing to accept that he was fallible, started to revile his generals as cowards if not traitors when things went wrong, insisting on taking even detailed decisions himself. This led to paralysis at the front line, where any troop movements in a backwards direction might incur the Führer's wrath for apparently retreating. Goebbels, visiting Hitler in March, found him 'greatly aged' and 'grave and withdrawn'. From this time Hitler began to degenerate physically and mentally, complaining of bouts of giddiness and stomach cramps. Instead of dividing much of his time between the spacious Berlin Chancellory and the Berghof, his Alpine eyrie, as earlier, he now closeted himself at Wolfsschanze (wolf's lair), his grim East Prussian headquarters, seldom even emerging for fresh air.

But with spring Hitler, convinced that his resolve alone had saved the situation that winter, recovered his self-confidence to plan fresh offensives. Boosted by 52 divisions from Hungary, Italy and the other 'satellites', this would capture the oil-rich Caucasus. 'If I do not get Maikop and Grozny (oil fields), I shall have to end this war,' he announced (Hitler, Adolf *Table Talk*, 1952). The key was the great industrial city of Stalingrad (Volgagrad) spread along the River Volga. Stalin, grown over-confident, ordered an ill-prepared offensive in May to recapture Kharkov, a major rail junction. The Germans, still tactically superior, trapped the Russians by a feigned retreat, inflicting huge casualties. Then Manstein's forces repelled a Soviet attack in the Crimea, on 4 July capturing Sevastopol after a long siege.

On 28 June the new German offensive, 'Operation Blue', began, again catching the Russians by surprise. (Stalin had spurned warnings that British intelligence, using Ultra, had given him.) The Russian line again crumpled in the face of Panzer and dive-bomber attacks and the important city of Rostov fell with hardly a fight on 23 July. As panic spread among the Russians, Stalin issued his famous 'Not one step back!' order but the German Sixth Army, commanded by General Paulus, still drove on, reaching the outskirts of Stalingrad on 19 August. Hitler was in jubilant mood once more, convinced that this time he had defeated the Russian colossus. From his advance HQ at Vinnitsa in Ukraine, he fatally divided his forces, sending Manstein's army north to help besiege Leningrad. The First Panzer Army was sent south towards the Caucasus. It reached the Maikop oil fields on 9 August to find them destroyed and an impenetrable line of fortifications along the Caucasus. These advances left the Sixth Army's extended flanks perilously exposed to counter-attacks, but Hitler dismissed any threats, saying that the Russians were finished.

In the Mediterranean, too, that spring the Germans took the offensive. Hitler had sent U-boat and air reinforcements to Italy in late 1941 to help Rommel overcome crippling supply problems, caused by aircraft and submarines operating from Malta, 'Britain's unsinkable aircraft-carrier' between Italy and Libya. Admiral Raeder urged Hitler to order the capture of Malta, vividly describing the prospect of the Afrika Korps driving east through Egypt to Iran, from which Germany could attack southern Russia. But as taking Malta required an expensive amphibious action, Hitler prevaricated, ordering only an air bombardment that almost, but not quite, subdued the island. It did reduce British operations from it, allowing Rommel, with a better supplied army, to capture Tobruk on 20 June, taking 35,000 prisoners and vital fuel. On 30 June the Afrika Korps reached El Alamein, only 80 miles (130 km) from Alexandria, but there halted through lack of reinforcements. The 'First Battle of El Alamein' in July created a stalemate, and both sides changed generals – the Germans losing Rommel on sick leave, the British gaining Montgomery, who slowly built up his forces. Hitler, never interested in the Mediterranean compared to Russia, had let slip a golden opportunity to rout the still weak British.

On the Eastern Front the battle for Stalingrad became crucial for both sides. A major communications centre, the city also had, through the Soviet dictator's name, great symbolic value. Hitler talked of it and Leningrad as the 'two holy cities of Communism' and devoted much military strength to trying to capture both. On 23 August, as German troops attacked Stalingrad's outskirts, the Luftwaffe launched a 600-bomber attack on it, creating fire storms that killed 40,000 people. But they also created ideal conditions, among the rubble and ruins, for defensive action against an enemy with more tanks – the Germans had four times as many at first. Later bombardments intensified the ruination, producing an infernally desolate landscape.

Throughout September and October the Germans fought their way street by ruined street, block by block, through Stalingrad. At times Germans would occupy the upper floors of a devastated building whose basement was still held by Russians. Fighting even went on in the sewers. Facing the Germans were not just regular troops but women, turning their anti-aircraft guns against Panzers. Bogged down in rubble, German troops lost the mobility essential to their success, despite capturing 90 per cent of the city by early November. Paulus, aware of Sixth Army's vulnerability to being cut off by Russian counter-attacks, wanted to withdraw but Hitler refused. When shown figures indicating that Stalin could muster huge forces and that Russian tank production had reached 1,200 per month, Hitler flew into a rage, foaming at the mouth, and forbade the messenger to read 'such idiotic twaddle' (Halder, Franz *Hitler as Warlord*, 1950). By late September relations between Hitler and his generals were so bad that Hitler took to having his meals on his own, refusing even to shake hands.

On 19 November three Russian Army Groups attacked. Undetected, indeed unsuspected by the Germans, they had massed a million men, 970 tanks and 1,350 aircraft, with 14,000 heavy guns on either side of the German position. Breaking through weak Axis lines, within five days they had encircled 220,000 German troops in Stalingrad. Hitler still refused to let the Sixth Army retreat, accepting Göring's lying assurance that the Luftwaffe could suply it. 'I will not pull back from the Volga!' he cried (Halder, 1950). Instead, the Sixth Army was to stand and fight to the last man. Manstein's attempts to break through and relieve it in December failed, and the Russian noose tightened around the starving army as winter deepened. The Russians expected them to surrender but they fought on until 31 January 1943, when some 90,000 men, all that remained of the 300,000 who had reached Stalingrad in August, finally surrendered. The loss of a whole army stunned Germany, and funeral music was played on the radio all day. Hitler's chief reaction was to berate Paulus for failing to commit suicide as ordered: 'The individual must die anyway. Beyond the life of the individual is the Nation … What hurts me most personally is that I promoted him to Field Marshal … That's the last Field Marshal I shall promote in this war!' (Gilbert, Felix *Hitler Directs His War*, 1954).

In Africa, too, the tide turned against the Germans. Montgomery, after building up Britain's Eighth Army to twice the strength of the German–Italian forces, attacked at El Alamein on 24 October, breaking through Axis lines and driving them east. Rommel could only mastermind a retreat. On 7 November Anglo–American forces landed along the coast of Morocco and Algeria, occupying the whole area quickly. Rommel appealed to Hitler to evacuate the Afrika Korps to Italy. Hitler, threatening Rommel with court-martial for daring even to suggest retreat, instead poured reinforcements into Tunisia – 75,000 German troops which might have conquered Egypt earlier. Rommel used them to maul the Allies at the Kasserine Pass in February 1943 but had to retreat as Montgomery's army approached from the east. Bottled up in Tunis, 150,000 Axis troops surrendered on 12 May.

The prolonged defence of Stalingrad had enabled German troops in the Caucasus to retreat with relatively few losses and Manstein extricated most troops further north, even recapturing Kharkov in March. An uneasy lull then settled on the front during the muddy thaw. Hitler, chastened by Stalingrad, let his generals decide the next move. Manstein chose to attack the Russian position at Kursk, precisely where the Russians had concentrated their forces, hoping to smash them and drive east again. When finally launched in July this proved the biggest tank battle in history: the Germans fielded 900,000 men and 3,000 tanks, many heavy new 'Tigers', but the Russians had prepared six concentric lines of defence manned by over a million men with 3,500 tanks, mostly formidable T-34s. After a week's bloody fighting the Germans were halted and the Russians attacked along the whole front. On 23 August they retook Kharkov, and by 6 November they had taken Kiev. The Germans, who had lost 500,000 men at Kursk, never launched another offensive in the East. Other fronts now demanded increasing attention as the 'Two-Front War' became reality.

On 10 July 1943 the Allies landed in Sicily, soon capturing it. This led to Mussolini's fall on 25 July, and a new Italian government began secret negotiations with the Allies to change sides, finally doing so on 13 October. Hitler, alarmed at the possible loss of all Italy, ordered the rescue of Mussolini – a daring mountain-top exploit by the SS – and told Kesselring,the German comander, to establish a line north of

Florence with 16 divisions. In fact, the Allies cautiously landed at Salerno in the south, and Kesselring easily established a 'Winter Line' beneath Rome, checking their advance until spring. But Hitler was now fighting on two land fronts as well by sea and air.

In December 1942 the Ultra team at Bletchley finally cracked the U-boats' Enigma code, enabling them to read German naval signals. Coupled with improved radar and depth charges, and by March 1943 long-range air patrols to cover the whole ocean, this turned the Battle of the Atlantic permanently in the Allies' favour. Although by early 1943 there were more U-boats in service than ever (212), Allied shipping losses fell while U-boat losses rose. At the same time the Allied bomber offensive began to hammer Germany. The RAF intensified its night-time raids on the Ruhr cities and Hamburg and began bombing Berlin, while the USAAF began daylight raids – riskier but more accurate – on industrial sites like Schweinfurt, centre of the aero-engine industry, in August 1943.

Germany's continued ability to fight, despite huge losses in men and material, was mainly due to the efforts of Hitler's youngest, most energetic minister, Albert Speer. Appointed Minister of Arms Production in February 1942, he galvanized the whole economy. This, despite Nazi rhetoric, had not so far been mobilized for war, and contained plenty of slack. Until late 1941 the production of consumer goods had continued to increase and very few women were working. Speer introduced bright young experts into the ministry and, with Hitler's backing, set ups special 'Speer teams' to streamline production. Speer's efforts were amazingly effective. German tank production rose from 5,200 in 1941 to 27,300 in 1944 – but Soviet tank production in 1944, from the many Russian factories which had been transported east in 1941, was even greater at 29,000. In the same period German aircraft production rose from under 12,000 to almost 40,000, the same as Russia's. (There was almost no fuel by late 1944 for the Luftwaffe, however, as Allied bombers had destroyed Germany's synthetic oil refineries and the Russians had overrun Romania's oil fields.) But the

US produced more aircraft than *all* other belligerent states combined during the war. Germany's three prime enemies – the US, the Soviet Union and the British empire – between them accounted for 75 per cent of world industrial production, and it was at last being brought to bear on the Reich. Despite increasingly voiced desires for peace, Hitler refused to contemplate peace negotiations, convinced that the 'unnatural' alliance of Communists and capitalists against him would fall apart and that 'secret weapons' would regain the initiative for Germany.

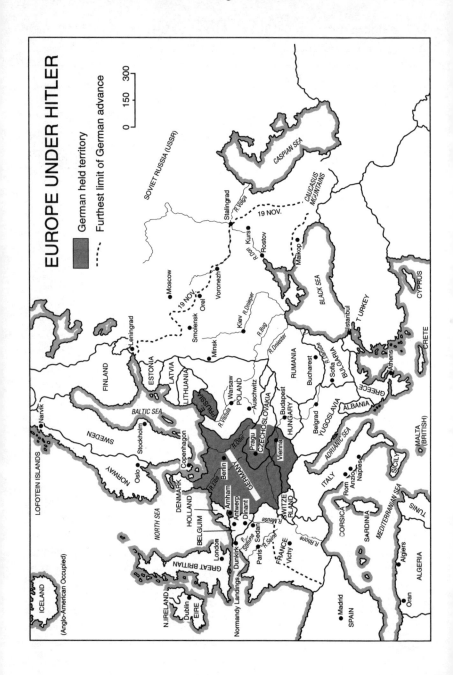

The last act

At the beginning of 1944, Russian armies crossed the River Dnieper and pushed on towards Poland, Allied bombers pounded Germany round the clock – the Americans began daytime bombing of Berlin in March 1944 – and an Allied invasion of northern France loomed. But Hitler remained confident. The Allied landings in North Africa and Italy had only succeeded because of treachery, he announced, which would not recur in France. Here a 'West Wall' of fortifications covering the coasts would repel invasion. Even if Allied forces landed, they could not be supplied for the Germans held the ports. Meanwhile, secret weapons would terrify the British, forcing them to sue for peace. With the threat in the West ended, Hitler could switch all troops and aircraft east to defeat the Russians.

Hitler's reasoning, if self-deluding, was not completely groundless. His 'Vengeance weapons' – revenge for the bombing of Germany – consisted of a pilotless jet aircraft, the V-1, launched from a ramp and carrying 700 kg of explosive, and the V-2, the world's first ballistic missile, with a one-ton warhead. If launched against London in the numbers planned (9,000 per month), landing at any hour, V-weapons might have proved devastating. But the RAF, informed by Polish resistance, bombed development sites at Peenemünde on the Baltic in August 1943, delaying production. Heavier attacks were made on the V-1's launching sites in northern France early in 1944. As a result, V-1 launches only started in June 1944 on a much reduced scale. Even so, they badly damaged London, causing 6,000 civilian casualties in June alone, before their sites were overrun in early September. The V-2 needed no launching site and could not be shot down once fired because of its speed, but few were fired (less than 2,000) mostly against Antwerp, by then in Allied hands. (The 200,000 workers employed on these might have been better employed building the Me-262, the first jet fighter, so checking Allied bombers. But Hitler, prevaricating, ordered it to be built as a bomber instead. Very few saw service.)

On 6 June the Allied invasion of France began in Normandy, the long-awaited 'Second Front' with 37 American, British and Canadian divisions, carried by 5,000 vessels and supported by 12,000 aircraft. The Luftwaffe hardly resisted them, neither did the German navy, but on land 60 German divisions, including 11 Panzer divisions, waited from Holland to the Spanish frontier. Although Hitler and Rommel guessed that the Allies would land in Normandy, most generals were fooled by bogus radio broadcasts into thinking that the Calais region was the intended area. Typically indecisive, Hitler insisted on dividing his forces, keeping many divisions east of the Seine while letting Rommel strengthen the Normandy defences. As a result, the strongest German forces were in north-east France, cut off from Normandy by massive bombing which destroyed rail and road links across France.

By 18 June 629,000 Allied soldiers and 95,000 vehicles had been landed, by 29 July 1,666,000 men and 333,000 vehicles – this was the world's first fully mechanized army. They were supplied by two 'Mulberry' floating harbours, which obviated the immediate need to capture a port, and by 20 PLUTOs, 'Pipelines under the Ocean', supplying petroleum. Even so, the fighting against dug-in Germans was vicious. It took the British on the east a month to capture Caen, while in the west Cherbourg was only captured on 26 June by the Americans with its great harbour wrecked. But on 25 July the US general Bradley broke out of the Cotentin peninsula and struck west into Brittany, before turning to catch the Germans on their flank. Soon the whole German position in France was threatened.

Hitler had flown west to inspect this latest front on 17 June, summoning his commanders to a bunker in Soissons. According to one observer, Hitler looked 'worn and sleepless, playing nervously with his spectacles and an array of coloured pencils … He was the only one who sat, hunched on a stool, while the field marshals stood' (Speidel, Hans

We Defended Normandy, 1951). Rommel tried to persuade Hitler to end the war, but Hitler only talked wildly of his V-weapons and told him: 'Don't you worry about the future course of the war. Look after your own invasion front.' (Speidel, Hans, 1951) Later attempts by his generals to make him see the war was lost proved equally unsuccessful. The Führer's attitude – to keep fighting until the 'unnatural alliance' against him fell apart – was not for changing. Only a change of government, by force, could save Germany from disaster. A conspiracy to do so now came to long-delayed fruition.

Just two institutions in Nazi Germany had any hope of overthrowing Hitler: the SS, grown enormously powerful under Himmler, and the army. Himmler, cautiously sounded out by conspirators, did not completely reject proposals, but showed no enthusiasm, being still under Hitler's spell – he stood to attention when Hitler telephoned him. The army, traditionally obedient to the state, was also slow to act. As long as Hitler seemed to be winning the war with huge popular support, he looked unassailable. But after Stalingrad, as Hitler became increasingly paranoid, abusing and sacking generals who dared to disagree with him, the need to kill him spurred a disparate group of liberals, priests, trade unionists and army officers into contemplating action. The 'Kreisau Circle' consisted of high-minded, mystical thinkers who did little but had friendly contacts in the Abwehr, the German counter-intelligence service, which protected more active conspirators. Attempts by young officers such as Schabrendorf, on the staff of the sympathetic General von Tresckow, to blow up Hitler's plane in March 1943 failed because the bomb failed to explode – it was retrieved before discovery – and other attempts that year also failed through remarkably bad luck. In December 1943 General Oster, the conspiracy's chief supporter in the Abwehr, was forced to resign.

At this crucial stage Colonel Klaus von Stauffenberg joined the conspiracy. A war hero who had lost his left eye and right hand fighting in Tunisia, he was on the General Staff, with frequent access to Hitler. He injected vital energy into the plotting, offering to place a bomb by

Hitler while others commanding the 'Home Army', the reserve forces in Berlin, took over the capital and formed a government to negotiate peace. Again he had bad luck, his first two attempts in July failing because Hitler left before the bomb could be primed. But on 20 July he arrived at the Wolfsschanze, Hitler's eastern headquarters, determined to succeed. Putting his briefcase under the heavy table on which maps were spread, he slipped out. Moments later the bomb went off, blowing the roof off the building. Stauffenberg assumed Hitler had been killed – but he had not. The briefcase had been pushed against a massive concrete table leg which had shielded him. Although his eardrums were damaged and his legs burned, Hitler was alive. Meanwhile Stauffenberg had telephoned the conspirators in Berlin telling them to launch 'Valkyrie', the code name for the rising, before flying back.

In Berlin the conspirators dithered until Stauffenberg himself returned, four hours after the bomb blast, but by now it was too late. A keen Nazi persuaded Major Remer, the officer sent to arrest Goebbels, to telephone Wolfsschanze, where he heard Hitler's unmistakable voice and began arresting the conspirators instead. At 6.30 pm Goebbels broadcast that there had been an unsuccessful attempt on the Führer's life and then Hitler himself came on the air. Fear seized all involved. Stauffenberg was shot at once before Himmler turned up to organize the manhunt methodically. Hitler's revenge on the officer corps, which he had always disliked for what he deemed to be its cowardice and incompetence, was terrible. About 5,000 people, guilty by remotest association, were caught and tortured to death – a film was made of some hanging by piano wire from steel hooks for Hitler to gloat over – and trials continued to the end of the war. The SS now controlled almost every aspect of German life, as it had long wished.

But it could not control events at the front. By late July 'Bagration', the greatest Russian offensive yet, begun on 22 June, the anniversary of Barbarossa, had destroyed German Army Group Centre round Minsk, taking 350,000 prisoners – most destined to die in Siberia – and cut off an equally large force along the Baltic in Courland, before it reached the

Vistula. Meanwhile another Soviet offensive swept into Romania in August, which promptly changed sides, as did Bulgaria, and entered Yugoslavia, joining Tito's victorious partisans. At the other end Finland withdrew from the war. Hitler sacked more generals but, by forbidding retreat when possible, turned defeats into disasters. Only round Budapest and along the Vistula was the Soviet advance temporarily halted.

In the west, the Americans entered Brittany on 31 July and Patton's Third Army struck east for Le Mans, reaching Argentan on 16 August – south of the Germans, who had the Canadians to the north and the British to the west. To avoid being encircled at Falaise, German forces needed to retreat speedily behind the Seine, but Hitler, from his distant Prussian headquarters, ordered them instead to attack. The result was the annihilation of Germany's western forces. Field Marshal von Kluge, who had succeeded Rommel – wounded by an air attack and later forced to commit suicide because of suspected complicity in the Stauffenberg plot – killed himself on 15 August rather than face Hitler's wrath. Montgomery then broke out of Normandy and led British troops across northern France through Belgium to the Dutch frontier, while in the south US troops raced to Alsace, reaching the German frontier on 11 September. Paris was liberated on the 23 August by French troops. In Italy Allied troops entered Rome on 3 June and pushed slowly north, although Kesselring halted them at the 'Gothic Line' in northern Italy for the winter.

Meanwhile the Allied air offensive intensified. In September USAAF raids almost ended German synthetic oil output, although it recovered marginally later. Hitler, however, still refused to consider making peace. On 31 August Hitler told his generals, 'The time has not yet come for a political decision … Such moments come when you are having successes … But the time will come when the tension between the Allies will become so great that the break will occur.' On such thin hopes, plus the conviction that he owed his miraculous escape from the bomb to 'Providence', he relied. His health was very bad, worsened by the bomb blast, his unhealthy life underground and the ever-increasing drugs from Dr Morrell. At times he was too weak even to talk. But he alone still directed Germany's defence.

The British attempt to cross the Rhine at Arnhem in Holland in late September failed disastrously and stiff German resistance stopped the Allies opening the great port of Antwerp until late November. Transport problems hampered the further advance of their armies, with many ports still held by German outposts or wrecked. This autumn pause allowed Hitler to dream up one last offensive. For this he chose the Ardennes, scene of his great breakthrough in 1940, aiming to recapture Antwerp and split the Allied armies. Gathering 28 divisions, of which ten were Panzers, he drew up detailed plans with 'Not to be altered' in his own handwriting on them. His generals protested, urging that the troops instead be sent east to meet the coming Russian offensive. Hitler, 'a stooped figure with a pale and puffy face … his hands trembling', dismissed their estimates of Soviet strength as 'the biggest bluff since Genghis Khan'. On paper Hitler still commanded huge forces – 260 divisions, spread often in isolated pockets from Norway to the Balkans – but these were mostly 'ghost' divisions of a few hundred men. Hitler refused to dissolve exhausted divisions. Deploying them on a map gave him the illusion of power.

Launched at dawn on 16 December the last German offensive caught the Allies completely by surprise. Aided by bad weather which grounded Allied airforces, the columns advanced some distance. But they never even approached Antwerp, partly due to the heroic defence of Bastogne by the US 101st airborne division, which denied the Germans desperately needed fuel. Montgomery, given command of all Allied troops in the section, calmed initial panic and soon the Germans, facing much greater forces, were on the defensive once more. Another German offensive in Alsace proved equally ineffectual. These attacks consumed Germany's very last reserves of manpower and materials.

The last act in Hitler's, and Nazi Germany's, life was typically bloody. On 12 January the Russians launched an offensive which took them across the Vistula, capturing Silesia, with Germany's last unbombed industries, and on to the River Oder, where Stalin halted them. On 13/14 February the RAF and USAAF together destroyed Dresden, a target of minimal military importance but a great cultural centre filled with refugees; perhaps 135,000 civilians died in the ensuing fire storms, but its railways were working again within three days. In March the Allies crossed the Rhine and on 16 April the Russians resumed their advance towards Berlin with 2.5 million men, 6,250 tanks and 7,500 aircraft. Against them the Germans could muster only a million troops, mostly old men or boys, and 1,500 tanks.

Meanwhile Hitler had returned to his Berlin bunker beneath the Chancery for good as Germany faced being cut in half by its enemies. His own physical condition was deteriorating fast. According to a young officer Captain Boldt who now met Hitler for the first time, his 'head was slightly wobbling. His left arm hung slackly and his hand trembled a lot. There was an indescribable flickering glow in his eyes … All his movements were those of a senile man' (Boldt, Gerhard *In the Shelter with Hitler*, 1949). Hitler's dire condition echoed that of the nation he had led to defeat, but he blamed Germany, not himself, for the war's outcome. 'If the war is to be lost, the nation also must perish … This fate is inevitable …The nation has proved itself weak and the future belongs to the stronger eastern nation… Those who remain after the battle are of little value,' he told Speer on 19 March, ordering the destruction of everything – trains, lorries, bridges, factories – of value in Germany. Such manic nihilism was shared by Goebbels but Speer, appalled, refused to promulgate these orders. He had already tried unsuccessfully to kill Hitler by gassing the bunker – a change in design of the ventilator shafts again saved Hitler. Almost until the last Hitler dreamed of a fantastic turnabout in his fortunes, such as had saved his hero Frederick the Great facing total defeat in 1761. The news of Roosevelt's death on 12 April gave him sudden hope of a break in the coalition against him, but this soon collapsed.

On his 56th birthday the Nazi chiefs gathered for the last time in his bunker – Göring, Himmler, Ribbentrop, Speer, Goebbels. Most advised him to leave Berlin for the 'National Redoubt' in the Alps which, according to Nazi propaganda but not in reality, was being fortified for a last stand. But Hitler refused, determined to end his days in his doomed capital, where Eva Braun had joined him. Now his oldest cronies began taking their leave, most going off to try to negotiate separately with the Allies – Himmler chose the Nordic Swedes as intermediaries. News of such 'treacheries' provoked fresh wrath from Hitler but when Speer flew in to confess his own treachery on 23 April he was, surprisingly, forgiven. Hitler was already past caring.

On 29 April, as shells from nearby Russian guns fell on the Chancery gardens, Hitler finally married Eva Braun. The ceremony took place in the bunker's map room, Goebbels and Martin Bormann being witnesses. A few secretaries and guards joined them for a glass of champagne, then Hitler retired to dictate his will and political testament. This showed no signs of remorse, blaming the usual enemies, especially the Jews and the officer corps, for defeat. Surprisingly he appointed Admiral Doenitz, head of the navy for the last two years, as his successor, deleting his obvious heirs. On 30 April he said farewell to his staff, poisoned Blondi, his favourite Alsatian dog, and then took his wife into their private quarters. A few moments later a shot rang out and when the door was opened, Hitler was lying on the sofa, soaked in blood. He had shot himself after poisoning Eva. Their bodies were taken outside and burnt, the watchers giving the Hitler salute for the last time. The Third Reich survived its founder by just one week before its remaining leaders offered the still united alliance the unconditional surrender demanded.

Hitler's place in history seems secure, but it is a place beside the great destroyers and scourges of humanity such as Attila the Hun or Genghis Khan. Nothing positive came of his regime. It produced not German expansion over Eurasia but German contraction. German refugees streamed west by the million in 1945, abandoning lands that had been theirs for centuries. For over 40 years Germany itself was divided and only reunited in a democratic, capitalist state. Even the Final Solution was not final, for out of it came the state of Israel. Hitler had real talents – primarily as a demagogue and politican, able to spot and exploit others' weaknesses – but the giant flaws in his character overshadowed his achievements. He deserves his infamy as one of the most evil men in history.

FURTHER READING

Books by Hitler

Mein Kampf (My Struggle) English translation 1939
Table Talk (posthumously published) 1952

Books on Hitler

Bullock, Alan *Hitler, A Study in Tyranny* [revised] 1962
Calvacoressi, Peter, John Pritchard and Guy Wint *The Causes and Courses of the Second World War* [revised] 1989
Collotti, Enzo *Hitler and Nazism* 1999
Fest, Joachim *Hitler* 1974
Kershaw, Ian *Hitler 1889–1936, Hubris* 1998;
Kershaw Ian *Hitler 1936–45, Nemesis* 2000
Lukacs, John *The Hitler of History* 2000
Overy, Richard *Russia's War* 1998
Shirer, William L. *The Rise and Fall of the Third Reich* 1960
Wilmot, Chester *The Struggle for Europe* 1952

INDEX

ISAAC NEWTON – A BEGINNER'S GUIDE

Jane Jakeman

Isaac Newton – A Beginner's Guide introduces you to this 17th century genius. Explore how his scientific discoveries revolutionized our world and his philosophy changed our thought. Learn about Newton the scientist, philosopher, alchemist and respected public figure.

Jane Jakeman's lively text:

- describes Newton's background and the times he lived in
- explores his scientific ideas and their effect on our lives
- delves into the character of this great man
- examines the influence of Newton both in his own time and today.

GANDHI –
A BEGINNER'S GUIDE

Genevieve Blais

Gandhi – A Beginner's Guide invites you to take a glimpse into the life of this profound character. Follow his extraordinary quest for morality, justice and spirituality and discover how his strategy of passive resistance achieved social reform.

Genevieve Blais's compelling text investigates:

- Gandhi's background and the times he lived in
- Britain's role in the history of India
- the events leading up to and prior to the Salt March
- Gandhi's role in the independence of India, his assassination and legacy.

CHURCHILL –
A BEGINNER'S GUIDE

Nigel Rodgers

Churchill – A Beginner's Guide reveals the real Churchill behind the myth of one of the great figures in twentieth-century history. It follows the ups and downs of his often stormy career as soldier, writer and statesman. Learn how Churchill, a romantic and a rebel, fell out of favour many times before becoming Britain's greatest wartime leader in 1940. Churchill's defiant brilliance helped save Britain, and perhaps the world, from Nazi tyranny, to leave a near-mythical legacy.

Nigel Rodgers' fascinating text uncovers:

- the troubled childhood and youth of a rebel aristocrat
- Churchill's remarkable radicalism in a Liberal administration
- the wilderness years – Churchill is out of office but in the right about Hitler
- the hour of destiny – at last he becomes Prime Minister to rally the nation
- the legend – why the myth of the cigar-smoking great Englishman lives on.